Addition Facts: 0 _ _

A. 4   2   6   0   1   9   5   3
   + 4   + 0   + 3   + 2   + 4   + 4   + 6   +

B. 1   5   8   2   4   5   1   6   7   4
   + 0   + 8   + 8   + 6   + 3   + 3   + 3   + 2   + 0   + 2

C. 8   0   7   3   1   7   6   2   9   0
   + 2   + 6   + 1   + 4   + 9   + 8   + 5   + 5   + 1   + 0

D. 2   5   1   8   5   0   6   4   3   8
   + 4   + 2   + 8   + 7   + 7   + 5   + 9   + 1   + 6   + 1

E. 6   3   7   0   5   2   8   1   7   4
   + 4   + 3   + 9   + 1   + 0   + 3   + 0   + 2   + 7   + 9

F. 4   1   3   9   2   9   4   9   1   9
   + 0   + 1   + 2   + 3   + 9   + 9   + 6   + 0   + 7   + 5

G. 5   2   7   3   8   0   6   3   7   6
   + 9   + 8   + 6   + 9   + 6   + 8   + 1   + 1   + 5   + 8

H. 7   4   2   6   1   9   3   8   0   6
   + 2   + 5   + 7   + 7   + 6   + 2   + 8   + 5   + 9   + 0

I. 0   8   5   3   9   5   2   9   7   4
   + 3   + 9   + 1   + 0   + 8   + 4   + 2   + 6   + 4   + 8

J. 5   1   9   4   2   7   0   8   6   3
   + 5   + 5   + 7   + 7   + 1   + 3   + 4   + 4   + 6   + 7

Minutes					Score
1	2	3	4	5	

Name_____

A.	5 + 1	2 + 1	8 + 5	4 + 8	1 + 3	9 + 9	7 + 0	0 + 2	8 + 9	3 + 6
B.	3 + 2	1 + 1	0 + 6	8 + 0	5 + 8	2 + 0	6 + 1	9 + 3	1 + 9	7 + 9
C.	1 + 8	7 + 1	3 + 5	1 + 6	6 + 9	3 + 1	8 + 8	0 + 7	4 + 7	5 + 0
D.	0 + 8	3 + 9	9 + 5	2 + 5	7 + 8	1 + 0	5 + 5	6 + 6	4 + 3	0 + 4
E.	4 + 9	6 + 0	2 + 9	4 + 2	9 + 0	3 + 7	8 + 4	1 + 5	7 + 3	3 + 4
F.	2 + 6	5 + 7	3 + 8	6 + 2	0 + 1	7 + 2	2 + 4	9 + 8	5 + 4	2 + 8
G.	3 + 3	0 + 3	1 + 2	6 + 5	3 + 0	5 + 3	8 + 3	1 + 7	7 + 7	5 + 9
H.	9 + 7	4 + 6	2 + 2	7 + 5	9 + 6	4 + 1	9 + 2	6 + 4	0 + 9	8 + 7
I.	4 + 0	8 + 1	5 + 2	8 + 6	1 + 4	4 + 5	7 + 6	0 + 0	9 + 4	6 + 7
J.	6 + 3	0 + 5	6 + 8	5 + 6	2 + 7	9 + 1	7 + 4	4 + 4	8 + 2	2 + 3

Minutes

1	2	3	4	5

Score

A.
$$\begin{array}{r}0\\+\ 4\\\hline\end{array}\quad\begin{array}{r}3\\+\ 7\\\hline\end{array}\quad\begin{array}{r}6\\+\ 3\\\hline\end{array}\quad\begin{array}{r}1\\+\ 8\\\hline\end{array}\quad\begin{array}{r}8\\+\ 4\\\hline\end{array}\quad\begin{array}{r}5\\+\ 1\\\hline\end{array}\quad\begin{array}{r}0\\+\ 3\\\hline\end{array}\quad\begin{array}{r}7\\+\ 1\\\hline\end{array}\quad\begin{array}{r}2\\+\ 2\\\hline\end{array}\quad\begin{array}{r}1\\+\ 1\\\hline\end{array}$$

B.
$$\begin{array}{r}4\\+\ 5\\\hline\end{array}\quad\begin{array}{r}8\\+\ 5\\\hline\end{array}\quad\begin{array}{r}2\\+\ 5\\\hline\end{array}\quad\begin{array}{r}9\\+\ 4\\\hline\end{array}\quad\begin{array}{r}3\\+\ 1\\\hline\end{array}\quad\begin{array}{r}7\\+\ 0\\\hline\end{array}\quad\begin{array}{r}9\\+\ 1\\\hline\end{array}\quad\begin{array}{r}0\\+\ 8\\\hline\end{array}\quad\begin{array}{r}7\\+\ 7\\\hline\end{array}\quad\begin{array}{r}4\\+\ 6\\\hline\end{array}$$

C.
$$\begin{array}{r}5\\+\ 5\\\hline\end{array}\quad\begin{array}{r}1\\+\ 0\\\hline\end{array}\quad\begin{array}{r}8\\+\ 0\\\hline\end{array}\quad\begin{array}{r}0\\+\ 0\\\hline\end{array}\quad\begin{array}{r}9\\+\ 7\\\hline\end{array}\quad\begin{array}{r}6\\+\ 2\\\hline\end{array}\quad\begin{array}{r}1\\+\ 7\\\hline\end{array}\quad\begin{array}{r}8\\+\ 3\\\hline\end{array}\quad\begin{array}{r}5\\+\ 4\\\hline\end{array}\quad\begin{array}{r}3\\+\ 3\\\hline\end{array}$$

D.
$$\begin{array}{r}3\\+\ 2\\\hline\end{array}\quad\begin{array}{r}9\\+\ 9\\\hline\end{array}\quad\begin{array}{r}2\\+\ 0\\\hline\end{array}\quad\begin{array}{r}7\\+\ 6\\\hline\end{array}\quad\begin{array}{r}1\\+\ 2\\\hline\end{array}\quad\begin{array}{r}4\\+\ 0\\\hline\end{array}\quad\begin{array}{r}5\\+\ 9\\\hline\end{array}\quad\begin{array}{r}9\\+\ 0\\\hline\end{array}\quad\begin{array}{r}2\\+\ 4\\\hline\end{array}\quad\begin{array}{r}6\\+\ 5\\\hline\end{array}$$

E.
$$\begin{array}{r}3\\+\ 8\\\hline\end{array}\quad\begin{array}{r}1\\+\ 6\\\hline\end{array}\quad\begin{array}{r}4\\+\ 7\\\hline\end{array}\quad\begin{array}{r}9\\+\ 2\\\hline\end{array}\quad\begin{array}{r}4\\+\ 4\\\hline\end{array}\quad\begin{array}{r}2\\+\ 8\\\hline\end{array}\quad\begin{array}{r}0\\+\ 7\\\hline\end{array}\quad\begin{array}{r}7\\+\ 8\\\hline\end{array}\quad\begin{array}{r}5\\+\ 8\\\hline\end{array}\quad\begin{array}{r}0\\+\ 2\\\hline\end{array}$$

F.
$$\begin{array}{r}2\\+\ 3\\\hline\end{array}\quad\begin{array}{r}8\\+\ 6\\\hline\end{array}\quad\begin{array}{r}4\\+\ 2\\\hline\end{array}\quad\begin{array}{r}0\\+\ 9\\\hline\end{array}\quad\begin{array}{r}7\\+\ 5\\\hline\end{array}\quad\begin{array}{r}5\\+\ 0\\\hline\end{array}\quad\begin{array}{r}8\\+\ 9\\\hline\end{array}\quad\begin{array}{r}6\\+\ 9\\\hline\end{array}\quad\begin{array}{r}3\\+\ 0\\\hline\end{array}\quad\begin{array}{r}8\\+\ 2\\\hline\end{array}$$

G.
$$\begin{array}{r}6\\+\ 4\\\hline\end{array}\quad\begin{array}{r}0\\+\ 1\\\hline\end{array}\quad\begin{array}{r}7\\+\ 9\\\hline\end{array}\quad\begin{array}{r}5\\+\ 6\\\hline\end{array}\quad\begin{array}{r}3\\+\ 6\\\hline\end{array}\quad\begin{array}{r}6\\+\ 1\\\hline\end{array}\quad\begin{array}{r}5\\+\ 3\\\hline\end{array}\quad\begin{array}{r}2\\+\ 9\\\hline\end{array}\quad\begin{array}{r}8\\+\ 8\\\hline\end{array}\quad\begin{array}{r}6\\+\ 6\\\hline\end{array}$$

H.
$$\begin{array}{r}5\\+\ 7\\\hline\end{array}\quad\begin{array}{r}2\\+\ 1\\\hline\end{array}\quad\begin{array}{r}1\\+\ 5\\\hline\end{array}\quad\begin{array}{r}4\\+\ 1\\\hline\end{array}\quad\begin{array}{r}9\\+\ 6\\\hline\end{array}\quad\begin{array}{r}2\\+\ 7\\\hline\end{array}\quad\begin{array}{r}7\\+\ 2\\\hline\end{array}\quad\begin{array}{r}4\\+\ 9\\\hline\end{array}\quad\begin{array}{r}1\\+\ 4\\\hline\end{array}\quad\begin{array}{r}4\\+\ 3\\\hline\end{array}$$

I.
$$\begin{array}{r}1\\+\ 3\\\hline\end{array}\quad\begin{array}{r}7\\+\ 4\\\hline\end{array}\quad\begin{array}{r}9\\+\ 3\\\hline\end{array}\quad\begin{array}{r}0\\+\ 5\\\hline\end{array}\quad\begin{array}{r}8\\+\ 7\\\hline\end{array}\quad\begin{array}{r}6\\+\ 7\\\hline\end{array}\quad\begin{array}{r}9\\+\ 5\\\hline\end{array}\quad\begin{array}{r}3\\+\ 5\\\hline\end{array}\quad\begin{array}{r}8\\+\ 1\\\hline\end{array}\quad\begin{array}{r}6\\+\ 8\\\hline\end{array}$$

J.
$$\begin{array}{r}2\\+\ 6\\\hline\end{array}\quad\begin{array}{r}4\\+\ 8\\\hline\end{array}\quad\begin{array}{r}3\\+\ 4\\\hline\end{array}\quad\begin{array}{r}6\\+\ 0\\\hline\end{array}\quad\begin{array}{r}3\\+\ 9\\\hline\end{array}\quad\begin{array}{r}0\\+\ 6\\\hline\end{array}\quad\begin{array}{r}9\\+\ 8\\\hline\end{array}\quad\begin{array}{r}5\\+\ 2\\\hline\end{array}\quad\begin{array}{r}1\\+\ 9\\\hline\end{array}\quad\begin{array}{r}7\\+\ 3\\\hline\end{array}$$

Minutes

1	2	3	4	5

Score

A.
$\begin{array}{r} 1 \\ + 2 \\ \hline \end{array}$
$\begin{array}{r} 8 \\ + 8 \\ \hline \end{array}$
$\begin{array}{r} 3 \\ + 2 \\ \hline \end{array}$
$\begin{array}{r} 6 \\ + 2 \\ \hline \end{array}$
$\begin{array}{r} 3 \\ + 9 \\ \hline \end{array}$
$\begin{array}{r} 1 \\ + 1 \\ \hline \end{array}$
$\begin{array}{r} 2 \\ + 2 \\ \hline \end{array}$
$\begin{array}{r} 5 \\ + 6 \\ \hline \end{array}$
$\begin{array}{r} 0 \\ + 7 \\ \hline \end{array}$
$\begin{array}{r} 5 \\ + 1 \\ \hline \end{array}$

B.
$\begin{array}{r} 2 \\ + 1 \\ \hline \end{array}$
$\begin{array}{r} 4 \\ + 2 \\ \hline \end{array}$
$\begin{array}{r} 0 \\ + 0 \\ \hline \end{array}$
$\begin{array}{r} 7 \\ + 2 \\ \hline \end{array}$
$\begin{array}{r} 8 \\ + 9 \\ \hline \end{array}$
$\begin{array}{r} 2 \\ + 0 \\ \hline \end{array}$
$\begin{array}{r} 3 \\ + 1 \\ \hline \end{array}$
$\begin{array}{r} 7 \\ + 6 \\ \hline \end{array}$
$\begin{array}{r} 4 \\ + 8 \\ \hline \end{array}$
$\begin{array}{r} 2 \\ + 8 \\ \hline \end{array}$

C.
$\begin{array}{r} 6 \\ + 8 \\ \hline \end{array}$
$\begin{array}{r} 3 \\ + 6 \\ \hline \end{array}$
$\begin{array}{r} 7 \\ + 9 \\ \hline \end{array}$
$\begin{array}{r} 2 \\ + 5 \\ \hline \end{array}$
$\begin{array}{r} 8 \\ + 2 \\ \hline \end{array}$
$\begin{array}{r} 7 \\ + 1 \\ \hline \end{array}$
$\begin{array}{r} 3 \\ + 5 \\ \hline \end{array}$
$\begin{array}{r} 9 \\ + 2 \\ \hline \end{array}$
$\begin{array}{r} 0 \\ + 2 \\ \hline \end{array}$
$\begin{array}{r} 6 \\ + 7 \\ \hline \end{array}$

D.
$\begin{array}{r} 0 \\ + 5 \\ \hline \end{array}$
$\begin{array}{r} 8 \\ + 3 \\ \hline \end{array}$
$\begin{array}{r} 4 \\ + 9 \\ \hline \end{array}$
$\begin{array}{r} 7 \\ + 5 \\ \hline \end{array}$
$\begin{array}{r} 4 \\ + 5 \\ \hline \end{array}$
$\begin{array}{r} 1 \\ + 4 \\ \hline \end{array}$
$\begin{array}{r} 8 \\ + 6 \\ \hline \end{array}$
$\begin{array}{r} 2 \\ + 4 \\ \hline \end{array}$
$\begin{array}{r} 4 \\ + 1 \\ \hline \end{array}$
$\begin{array}{r} 1 \\ + 9 \\ \hline \end{array}$

E.
$\begin{array}{r} 6 \\ + 3 \\ \hline \end{array}$
$\begin{array}{r} 1 \\ + 3 \\ \hline \end{array}$
$\begin{array}{r} 9 \\ + 1 \\ \hline \end{array}$
$\begin{array}{r} 0 \\ + 8 \\ \hline \end{array}$
$\begin{array}{r} 5 \\ + 3 \\ \hline \end{array}$
$\begin{array}{r} 7 \\ + 7 \\ \hline \end{array}$
$\begin{array}{r} 5 \\ + 0 \\ \hline \end{array}$
$\begin{array}{r} 1 \\ + 0 \\ \hline \end{array}$
$\begin{array}{r} 3 \\ + 8 \\ \hline \end{array}$
$\begin{array}{r} 5 \\ + 8 \\ \hline \end{array}$

F.
$\begin{array}{r} 4 \\ + 6 \\ \hline \end{array}$
$\begin{array}{r} 8 \\ + 7 \\ \hline \end{array}$
$\begin{array}{r} 5 \\ + 5 \\ \hline \end{array}$
$\begin{array}{r} 7 \\ + 0 \\ \hline \end{array}$
$\begin{array}{r} 0 \\ + 4 \\ \hline \end{array}$
$\begin{array}{r} 6 \\ + 1 \\ \hline \end{array}$
$\begin{array}{r} 5 \\ + 7 \\ \hline \end{array}$
$\begin{array}{r} 6 \\ + 6 \\ \hline \end{array}$
$\begin{array}{r} 9 \\ + 7 \\ \hline \end{array}$
$\begin{array}{r} 0 \\ + 6 \\ \hline \end{array}$

G.
$\begin{array}{r} 2 \\ + 6 \\ \hline \end{array}$
$\begin{array}{r} 4 \\ + 0 \\ \hline \end{array}$
$\begin{array}{r} 2 \\ + 3 \\ \hline \end{array}$
$\begin{array}{r} 9 \\ + 0 \\ \hline \end{array}$
$\begin{array}{r} 3 \\ + 4 \\ \hline \end{array}$
$\begin{array}{r} 3 \\ + 0 \\ \hline \end{array}$
$\begin{array}{r} 1 \\ + 8 \\ \hline \end{array}$
$\begin{array}{r} 7 \\ + 4 \\ \hline \end{array}$
$\begin{array}{r} 4 \\ + 4 \\ \hline \end{array}$
$\begin{array}{r} 9 \\ + 5 \\ \hline \end{array}$

H.
$\begin{array}{r} 6 \\ + 0 \\ \hline \end{array}$
$\begin{array}{r} 7 \\ + 8 \\ \hline \end{array}$
$\begin{array}{r} 3 \\ + 7 \\ \hline \end{array}$
$\begin{array}{r} 1 \\ + 5 \\ \hline \end{array}$
$\begin{array}{r} 8 \\ + 5 \\ \hline \end{array}$
$\begin{array}{r} 2 \\ + 7 \\ \hline \end{array}$
$\begin{array}{r} 9 \\ + 9 \\ \hline \end{array}$
$\begin{array}{r} 0 \\ + 1 \\ \hline \end{array}$
$\begin{array}{r} 8 \\ + 1 \\ \hline \end{array}$
$\begin{array}{r} 6 \\ + 5 \\ \hline \end{array}$

I.
$\begin{array}{r} 6 \\ + 9 \\ \hline \end{array}$
$\begin{array}{r} 1 \\ + 6 \\ \hline \end{array}$
$\begin{array}{r} 3 \\ + 3 \\ \hline \end{array}$
$\begin{array}{r} 7 \\ + 3 \\ \hline \end{array}$
$\begin{array}{r} 5 \\ + 9 \\ \hline \end{array}$
$\begin{array}{r} 8 \\ + 0 \\ \hline \end{array}$
$\begin{array}{r} 4 \\ + 3 \\ \hline \end{array}$
$\begin{array}{r} 8 \\ + 4 \\ \hline \end{array}$
$\begin{array}{r} 9 \\ + 8 \\ \hline \end{array}$
$\begin{array}{r} 1 \\ + 7 \\ \hline \end{array}$

J.
$\begin{array}{r} 0 \\ + 3 \\ \hline \end{array}$
$\begin{array}{r} 9 \\ + 4 \\ \hline \end{array}$
$\begin{array}{r} 5 \\ + 2 \\ \hline \end{array}$
$\begin{array}{r} 2 \\ + 9 \\ \hline \end{array}$
$\begin{array}{r} 6 \\ + 4 \\ \hline \end{array}$
$\begin{array}{r} 4 \\ + 7 \\ \hline \end{array}$
$\begin{array}{r} 9 \\ + 3 \\ \hline \end{array}$
$\begin{array}{r} 0 \\ + 9 \\ \hline \end{array}$
$\begin{array}{r} 9 \\ + 6 \\ \hline \end{array}$
$\begin{array}{r} 5 \\ + 4 \\ \hline \end{array}$

Minutes | 1 | 2 | 3 | 4 | 5 |

Score

Name_____

A.
```
  1      9      3      0      9      5      2      8      6      1
+ 7    + 5    + 4    + 2    + 2    + 0    + 3    + 3    + 1    + 3
```

B.
```
  4      2      5      2      7      3      1      4      0      7
+ 9    + 9    + 8    + 0    + 7    + 9    + 9    + 1    + 7    + 4
```

C.
```
  7      0      8      4      8      1      6      3      5      4
+ 3    + 3    + 5    + 3    + 1    + 0    + 4    + 1    + 6    + 6
```

D.
```
  2      3      1      7      5      2      6      2      1      6
+ 4    + 5    + 2    + 6    + 3    + 8    + 0    + 2    + 8    + 9
```

E.
```
  0      6      4      7      0      9      4      9      2      3
+ 9    + 7    + 8    + 9    + 5    + 6    + 5    + 0    + 6    + 0
```

F.
```
  8      6      1      7      6      8      9      3      0      9
+ 4    + 8    + 6    + 5    + 3    + 9    + 8    + 3    + 1    + 3
```

G.
```
  3      0      5      3      8      1      7      6      5      6
+ 2    + 6    + 5    + 8    + 2    + 5    + 2    + 5    + 7    + 7
```

H.
```
  9      2      4      2      9      5      4      8      0      8
+ 9    + 7    + 0    + 1    + 7    + 2    + 2    + 8    + 8    + 6
```

I.
```
  4      0      5      4      8      7      9      3      7      5
+ 4    + 0    + 9    + 7    + 7    + 1    + 1    + 7    + 8    + 4
```

J.
```
  5      7      1      8      1      6      3      2      9      0
+ 1    + 0    + 4    + 0    + 1    + 2    + 6    + 5    + 4    + 4
```

Minutes

1	2	3	4	5

Score

© Carson-Dellosa Publ. CD-0901

A. 4 + 7	8 + 2	0 + 8	6 + 3	4 + 2	3 + 5	9 + 0	1 + 1	7 + 6	5 + 4
B. 9 + 4	2 + 2	5 + 5	1 + 5	6 + 9	7 + 5	2 + 5	9 + 6	0 + 4	3 + 0
C. 0 + 0	8 + 5	4 + 6	6 + 2	1 + 0	8 + 7	5 + 2	2 + 7	6 + 8	3 + 8
D. 4 + 3	1 + 4	3 + 1	7 + 1	5 + 8	0 + 2	2 + 1	7 + 4	1 + 3	4 + 5
E. 3 + 7	3 + 4	5 + 3	0 + 5	9 + 7	8 + 1	5 + 7	1 + 7	8 + 4	6 + 1
F. 0 + 9	6 + 4	4 + 0	3 + 6	1 + 9	7 + 0	6 + 7	2 + 4	9 + 2	0 + 7
G. 3 + 2	7 + 3	2 + 6	6 + 6	8 + 0	1 + 2	8 + 6	4 + 4	8 + 9	7 + 7
H. 2 + 3	0 + 3	9 + 8	4 + 8	6 + 0	5 + 6	3 + 3	5 + 1	0 + 1	9 + 5
I. 4 + 9	8 + 3	2 + 9	9 + 1	3 + 9	6 + 5	1 + 6	7 + 8	9 + 9	5 + 0
J. 1 + 8	4 + 1	7 + 2	0 + 6	7 + 9	2 + 8	8 + 8	5 + 9	2 + 0	9 + 3

Minutes   **Score**

1	2	3	4	5	

A.
$\begin{array}{r}3\\+\ 2\\\hline\end{array}$
$\begin{array}{r}0\\+\ 3\\\hline\end{array}$
$\begin{array}{r}5\\+\ 2\\\hline\end{array}$
$\begin{array}{r}6\\+\ 1\\\hline\end{array}$
$\begin{array}{r}3\\+\ 7\\\hline\end{array}$
$\begin{array}{r}2\\+\ 7\\\hline\end{array}$
$\begin{array}{r}8\\+\ 6\\\hline\end{array}$
$\begin{array}{r}4\\+\ 2\\\hline\end{array}$
$\begin{array}{r}1\\+\ 2\\\hline\end{array}$
$\begin{array}{r}2\\+\ 0\\\hline\end{array}$

B.
$\begin{array}{r}7\\+\ 7\\\hline\end{array}$
$\begin{array}{r}5\\+\ 5\\\hline\end{array}$
$\begin{array}{r}2\\+\ 2\\\hline\end{array}$
$\begin{array}{r}6\\+\ 5\\\hline\end{array}$
$\begin{array}{r}1\\+\ 1\\\hline\end{array}$
$\begin{array}{r}9\\+\ 2\\\hline\end{array}$
$\begin{array}{r}3\\+\ 1\\\hline\end{array}$
$\begin{array}{r}7\\+\ 2\\\hline\end{array}$
$\begin{array}{r}0\\+\ 0\\\hline\end{array}$
$\begin{array}{r}4\\+\ 9\\\hline\end{array}$

C.
$\begin{array}{r}4\\+\ 8\\\hline\end{array}$
$\begin{array}{r}8\\+\ 9\\\hline\end{array}$
$\begin{array}{r}0\\+\ 7\\\hline\end{array}$
$\begin{array}{r}9\\+\ 4\\\hline\end{array}$
$\begin{array}{r}5\\+\ 1\\\hline\end{array}$
$\begin{array}{r}8\\+\ 0\\\hline\end{array}$
$\begin{array}{r}6\\+\ 9\\\hline\end{array}$
$\begin{array}{r}1\\+\ 9\\\hline\end{array}$
$\begin{array}{r}2\\+\ 4\\\hline\end{array}$
$\begin{array}{r}4\\+\ 6\\\hline\end{array}$

D.
$\begin{array}{r}9\\+\ 0\\\hline\end{array}$
$\begin{array}{r}1\\+\ 3\\\hline\end{array}$
$\begin{array}{r}8\\+\ 2\\\hline\end{array}$
$\begin{array}{r}3\\+\ 0\\\hline\end{array}$
$\begin{array}{r}2\\+\ 6\\\hline\end{array}$
$\begin{array}{r}3\\+\ 6\\\hline\end{array}$
$\begin{array}{r}1\\+\ 6\\\hline\end{array}$
$\begin{array}{r}7\\+\ 6\\\hline\end{array}$
$\begin{array}{r}0\\+\ 2\\\hline\end{array}$
$\begin{array}{r}5\\+\ 8\\\hline\end{array}$

E.
$\begin{array}{r}2\\+\ 1\\\hline\end{array}$
$\begin{array}{r}3\\+\ 3\\\hline\end{array}$
$\begin{array}{r}9\\+\ 7\\\hline\end{array}$
$\begin{array}{r}4\\+\ 1\\\hline\end{array}$
$\begin{array}{r}0\\+\ 5\\\hline\end{array}$
$\begin{array}{r}5\\+\ 4\\\hline\end{array}$
$\begin{array}{r}5\\+\ 0\\\hline\end{array}$
$\begin{array}{r}1\\+\ 0\\\hline\end{array}$
$\begin{array}{r}6\\+\ 4\\\hline\end{array}$
$\begin{array}{r}3\\+\ 9\\\hline\end{array}$

F.
$\begin{array}{r}2\\+\ 5\\\hline\end{array}$
$\begin{array}{r}0\\+\ 1\\\hline\end{array}$
$\begin{array}{r}7\\+\ 3\\\hline\end{array}$
$\begin{array}{r}7\\+\ 0\\\hline\end{array}$
$\begin{array}{r}4\\+\ 4\\\hline\end{array}$
$\begin{array}{r}6\\+\ 0\\\hline\end{array}$
$\begin{array}{r}2\\+\ 9\\\hline\end{array}$
$\begin{array}{r}7\\+\ 9\\\hline\end{array}$
$\begin{array}{r}6\\+\ 8\\\hline\end{array}$
$\begin{array}{r}1\\+\ 4\\\hline\end{array}$

G.
$\begin{array}{r}8\\+\ 4\\\hline\end{array}$
$\begin{array}{r}3\\+\ 8\\\hline\end{array}$
$\begin{array}{r}6\\+\ 3\\\hline\end{array}$
$\begin{array}{r}1\\+\ 8\\\hline\end{array}$
$\begin{array}{r}9\\+\ 3\\\hline\end{array}$
$\begin{array}{r}4\\+\ 7\\\hline\end{array}$
$\begin{array}{r}3\\+\ 5\\\hline\end{array}$
$\begin{array}{r}9\\+\ 9\\\hline\end{array}$
$\begin{array}{r}0\\+\ 6\\\hline\end{array}$
$\begin{array}{r}9\\+\ 6\\\hline\end{array}$

H.
$\begin{array}{r}6\\+\ 6\\\hline\end{array}$
$\begin{array}{r}5\\+\ 6\\\hline\end{array}$
$\begin{array}{r}8\\+\ 7\\\hline\end{array}$
$\begin{array}{r}4\\+\ 0\\\hline\end{array}$
$\begin{array}{r}2\\+\ 3\\\hline\end{array}$
$\begin{array}{r}9\\+\ 8\\\hline\end{array}$
$\begin{array}{r}8\\+\ 3\\\hline\end{array}$
$\begin{array}{r}0\\+\ 9\\\hline\end{array}$
$\begin{array}{r}8\\+\ 5\\\hline\end{array}$
$\begin{array}{r}5\\+\ 7\\\hline\end{array}$

I.
$\begin{array}{r}7\\+\ 1\\\hline\end{array}$
$\begin{array}{r}1\\+\ 5\\\hline\end{array}$
$\begin{array}{r}7\\+\ 5\\\hline\end{array}$
$\begin{array}{r}7\\+\ 8\\\hline\end{array}$
$\begin{array}{r}8\\+\ 1\\\hline\end{array}$
$\begin{array}{r}0\\+\ 4\\\hline\end{array}$
$\begin{array}{r}6\\+\ 2\\\hline\end{array}$
$\begin{array}{r}2\\+\ 8\\\hline\end{array}$
$\begin{array}{r}7\\+\ 4\\\hline\end{array}$
$\begin{array}{r}9\\+\ 1\\\hline\end{array}$

J.
$\begin{array}{r}3\\+\ 4\\\hline\end{array}$
$\begin{array}{r}5\\+\ 9\\\hline\end{array}$
$\begin{array}{r}4\\+\ 5\\\hline\end{array}$
$\begin{array}{r}0\\+\ 8\\\hline\end{array}$
$\begin{array}{r}9\\+\ 5\\\hline\end{array}$
$\begin{array}{r}5\\+\ 3\\\hline\end{array}$
$\begin{array}{r}4\\+\ 3\\\hline\end{array}$
$\begin{array}{r}8\\+\ 8\\\hline\end{array}$
$\begin{array}{r}1\\+\ 7\\\hline\end{array}$
$\begin{array}{r}6\\+\ 7\\\hline\end{array}$

Minutes

1	2	3	4	5

Score

A.
$$\begin{array}{r}2\\+7\\\hline\end{array}\quad\begin{array}{r}9\\+4\\\hline\end{array}\quad\begin{array}{r}6\\+6\\\hline\end{array}\quad\begin{array}{r}1\\+6\\\hline\end{array}\quad\begin{array}{r}3\\+0\\\hline\end{array}\quad\begin{array}{r}8\\+2\\\hline\end{array}\quad\begin{array}{r}2\\+0\\\hline\end{array}\quad\begin{array}{r}9\\+7\\\hline\end{array}\quad\begin{array}{r}0\\+2\\\hline\end{array}\quad\begin{array}{r}3\\+5\\\hline\end{array}$$

B.
$$\begin{array}{r}3\\+6\\\hline\end{array}\quad\begin{array}{r}1\\+0\\\hline\end{array}\quad\begin{array}{r}8\\+5\\\hline\end{array}\quad\begin{array}{r}4\\+6\\\hline\end{array}\quad\begin{array}{r}7\\+0\\\hline\end{array}\quad\begin{array}{r}0\\+7\\\hline\end{array}\quad\begin{array}{r}9\\+5\\\hline\end{array}\quad\begin{array}{r}5\\+2\\\hline\end{array}\quad\begin{array}{r}7\\+6\\\hline\end{array}\quad\begin{array}{r}2\\+5\\\hline\end{array}$$

C.
$$\begin{array}{r}7\\+8\\\hline\end{array}\quad\begin{array}{r}4\\+0\\\hline\end{array}\quad\begin{array}{r}1\\+9\\\hline\end{array}\quad\begin{array}{r}0\\+0\\\hline\end{array}\quad\begin{array}{r}9\\+3\\\hline\end{array}\quad\begin{array}{r}6\\+4\\\hline\end{array}\quad\begin{array}{r}3\\+4\\\hline\end{array}\quad\begin{array}{r}8\\+9\\\hline\end{array}\quad\begin{array}{r}1\\+4\\\hline\end{array}\quad\begin{array}{r}6\\+5\\\hline\end{array}$$

D.
$$\begin{array}{r}0\\+6\\\hline\end{array}\quad\begin{array}{r}7\\+1\\\hline\end{array}\quad\begin{array}{r}6\\+3\\\hline\end{array}\quad\begin{array}{r}2\\+1\\\hline\end{array}\quad\begin{array}{r}5\\+3\\\hline\end{array}\quad\begin{array}{r}1\\+1\\\hline\end{array}\quad\begin{array}{r}7\\+7\\\hline\end{array}\quad\begin{array}{r}5\\+9\\\hline\end{array}\quad\begin{array}{r}2\\+4\\\hline\end{array}\quad\begin{array}{r}8\\+4\\\hline\end{array}$$

E.
$$\begin{array}{r}1\\+8\\\hline\end{array}\quad\begin{array}{r}8\\+3\\\hline\end{array}\quad\begin{array}{r}4\\+2\\\hline\end{array}\quad\begin{array}{r}8\\+0\\\hline\end{array}\quad\begin{array}{r}2\\+9\\\hline\end{array}\quad\begin{array}{r}9\\+9\\\hline\end{array}\quad\begin{array}{r}0\\+1\\\hline\end{array}\quad\begin{array}{r}7\\+3\\\hline\end{array}\quad\begin{array}{r}4\\+7\\\hline\end{array}\quad\begin{array}{r}1\\+5\\\hline\end{array}$$

F.
$$\begin{array}{r}7\\+5\\\hline\end{array}\quad\begin{array}{r}1\\+3\\\hline\end{array}\quad\begin{array}{r}5\\+4\\\hline\end{array}\quad\begin{array}{r}4\\+1\\\hline\end{array}\quad\begin{array}{r}0\\+5\\\hline\end{array}\quad\begin{array}{r}8\\+8\\\hline\end{array}\quad\begin{array}{r}3\\+7\\\hline\end{array}\quad\begin{array}{r}9\\+8\\\hline\end{array}\quad\begin{array}{r}4\\+3\\\hline\end{array}\quad\begin{array}{r}6\\+9\\\hline\end{array}$$

G.
$$\begin{array}{r}2\\+8\\\hline\end{array}\quad\begin{array}{r}9\\+1\\\hline\end{array}\quad\begin{array}{r}6\\+2\\\hline\end{array}\quad\begin{array}{r}3\\+2\\\hline\end{array}\quad\begin{array}{r}8\\+1\\\hline\end{array}\quad\begin{array}{r}4\\+8\\\hline\end{array}\quad\begin{array}{r}9\\+6\\\hline\end{array}\quad\begin{array}{r}0\\+9\\\hline\end{array}\quad\begin{array}{r}8\\+7\\\hline\end{array}\quad\begin{array}{r}5\\+8\\\hline\end{array}$$

H.
$$\begin{array}{r}4\\+9\\\hline\end{array}\quad\begin{array}{r}6\\+7\\\hline\end{array}\quad\begin{array}{r}0\\+4\\\hline\end{array}\quad\begin{array}{r}5\\+5\\\hline\end{array}\quad\begin{array}{r}4\\+4\\\hline\end{array}\quad\begin{array}{r}1\\+2\\\hline\end{array}\quad\begin{array}{r}5\\+0\\\hline\end{array}\quad\begin{array}{r}2\\+3\\\hline\end{array}\quad\begin{array}{r}9\\+2\\\hline\end{array}\quad\begin{array}{r}3\\+8\\\hline\end{array}$$

I.
$$\begin{array}{r}3\\+3\\\hline\end{array}\quad\begin{array}{r}7\\+2\\\hline\end{array}\quad\begin{array}{r}5\\+6\\\hline\end{array}\quad\begin{array}{r}6\\+0\\\hline\end{array}\quad\begin{array}{r}1\\+7\\\hline\end{array}\quad\begin{array}{r}7\\+4\\\hline\end{array}\quad\begin{array}{r}5\\+7\\\hline\end{array}\quad\begin{array}{r}9\\+0\\\hline\end{array}\quad\begin{array}{r}0\\+3\\\hline\end{array}\quad\begin{array}{r}6\\+8\\\hline\end{array}$$

J.
$$\begin{array}{r}4\\+5\\\hline\end{array}\quad\begin{array}{r}0\\+8\\\hline\end{array}\quad\begin{array}{r}6\\+1\\\hline\end{array}\quad\begin{array}{r}3\\+1\\\hline\end{array}\quad\begin{array}{r}2\\+2\\\hline\end{array}\quad\begin{array}{r}8\\+6\\\hline\end{array}\quad\begin{array}{r}5\\+1\\\hline\end{array}\quad\begin{array}{r}3\\+9\\\hline\end{array}\quad\begin{array}{r}7\\+9\\\hline\end{array}\quad\begin{array}{r}2\\+6\\\hline\end{array}$$

Minutes

1	2	3	4	5

Score

A.	5 + 5 =	1 + 4 =	3 + 8 =	8 + 5 =	1 + 0 =
B.	6 + 1 =	7 + 5 =	2 + 7 =	3 + 2 =	4 + 3 =
C.	0 + 5 =	7 + 1 =	5 + 2 =	0 + 2 =	5 + 9 =
D.	8 + 2 =	3 + 3 =	9 + 1 =	6 + 6 =	2 + 2 =
E.	8 + 9 =	4 + 2 =	0 + 4 =	5 + 4 =	1 + 8 =
F.	1 + 7 =	9 + 5 =	5 + 8 =	2 + 6 =	6 + 4 =
G.	2 + 8 =	0 + 9 =	6 + 0 =	7 + 4 =	3 + 5 =
H.	7 + 7 =	6 + 5 =	4 + 9 =	1 + 3 =	0 + 0 =
I.	5 + 3 =	4 + 5 =	3 + 0 =	8 + 1 =	4 + 1 =
J.	2 + 1 =	7 + 0 =	9 + 3 =	2 + 0 =	6 + 9 =
K.	8 + 6 =	0 + 1 =	5 + 0 =	8 + 4 =	1 + 6 =
L.	3 + 6 =	9 + 9 =	2 + 5 =	0 + 8 =	8 + 8 =
M.	8 + 0 =	3 + 9 =	7 + 9 =	6 + 3 =	5 + 7 =
N.	1 + 1 =	9 + 7 =	4 + 4 =	3 + 4 =	9 + 6 =
O.	9 + 2 =	2 + 3 =	7 + 3 =	4 + 0 =	0 + 7 =
P.	0 + 6 =	7 + 6 =	0 + 3 =	6 + 8 =	5 + 1 =
Q.	4 + 6 =	5 + 6 =	4 + 7 =	8 + 7 =	4 + 8 =
R.	7 + 2 =	3 + 1 =	9 + 0 =	2 + 9 =	9 + 4 =
S.	6 + 2 =	1 + 2 =	8 + 3 =	9 + 8 =	7 + 8 =
T.	1 + 5 =	6 + 7 =	3 + 7 =	1 + 9 =	2 + 4 =

Minutes

1	2	3	4	5

Score

A.	4 + 3 =	7 + 0 =	0 + 8 =	6 + 6 =	5 + 8 =
B.	7 + 5 =	2 + 4 =	7 + 7 =	3 + 1 =	0 + 2 =
C.	6 + 2 =	3 + 2 =	9 + 5 =	9 + 0 =	3 + 7 =
D.	0 + 9 =	5 + 5 =	4 + 0 =	2 + 6 =	8 + 6 =
E.	8 + 4 =	9 + 2 =	8 + 8 -	8 + 2 =	4 + 8 =
F.	4 + 9 =	0 + 3 =	3 + 8 =	1 + 0 =	7 + 9 =
G.	1 + 2 =	2 + 5 =	2 + 0 =	6 + 1 =	1 + 6 =
H.	9 + 9 =	6 + 5 =	5 + 3 =	3 + 6 =	6 + 8 =
I.	5 + 0 =	3 + 3 =	9 + 8 =	0 + 1 =	7 + 3 =
J.	1 + 9 =	5 + 7 =	1 + 5 =	7 + 6 =	2 + 2 =
K.	9 + 6 =	1 + 1 =	4 + 4 =	4 + 7 =	9 + 1 =
L.	0 + 5 =	7 + 4 =	2 + 8 =	0 + 7 =	5 + 4 =
M.	7 + 1 =	8 + 7 =	3 + 0 =	6 + 3 =	0 + 4 =
N.	3 + 9 =	2 + 1 =	2 + 3 =	4 + 2 =	9 + 4 =
O.	3 + 5 =	6 + 7 =	1 + 4 =	8 + 1 =	5 + 2 =
P.	6 + 0 =	0 + 0 =	8 + 5 =	2 + 7 =	1 + 8 =
Q.	7 + 8 =	5 + 1 =	4 + 6 =	7 + 2 =	3 + 4 =
R.	1 + 3 =	9 + 7 =	8 + 9 =	5 + 9 =	8 + 3 =
S.	5 + 6 =	8 + 0 =	0 + 6 =	9 + 3 =	6 + 4 =
T.	4 + 5 =	2 + 9 =	6 + 9 =	1 + 7 =	4 + 1 =

Minutes

1	2	3	4	5

Score

A.	5 + 4 =	2 + 0 =	1 + 4 =	6 + 2 =	3 + 0 =
B.	8 + 0 =	9 + 2 =	8 + 2 =	5 + 1 =	9 + 6 =
C.	0 + 4 =	7 + 2 =	6 + 7 =	2 + 9 =	0 + 2 =
D.	8 + 5 =	3 + 4 =	9 + 9 =	1 + 0 =	7 + 4 =
E.	1 + 5 =	9 + 4 =	0 + 7 =	3 + 8 =	4 + 2 =
F.	7 + 6 =	0 + 1 =	3 + 3 =	8 + 7 =	1 + 3 =
G.	4 + 5 =	2 + 1 =	2 + 8 =	7 + 0 =	5 + 3 =
H.	6 + 1 =	7 + 9 =	4 + 1 =	1 + 6 =	2 + 2 =
I.	1 + 7 =	5 + 7 =	6 + 0 =	4 + 6 =	3 + 5 =
J.	5 + 2 =	6 + 8 =	1 + 2 =	8 + 8 =	0 + 6 =
K.	3 + 7 =	0 + 8 =	2 + 3 =	5 + 6 =	5 + 9 =
L.	9 + 7 =	4 + 4 =	5 + 0 =	9 + 5 =	7 + 8 =
M.	1 + 1 =	2 + 6 =	7 + 5 =	0 + 0 =	9 + 1 =
N.	4 + 0 =	6 + 5 =	3 + 6 =	6 + 4 =	4 + 8 =
O.	7 + 1 =	4 + 7 =	9 + 3 =	3 + 9 =	8 + 3 =
P.	2 + 7 =	8 + 6 =	0 + 5 =	7 + 7 =	2 + 5 =
Q.	8 + 1 =	0 + 3 =	8 + 4 =	9 + 8 =	1 + 9 =
R.	5 + 5 =	6 + 9 =	4 + 9 =	4 + 3 =	3 + 2 =
S.	8 + 9 =	3 + 1 =	9 + 0 =	6 + 6 =	7 + 3 =
T.	0 + 9 =	6 + 3 =	2 + 4 =	1 + 8 =	5 + 8 =

Minutes   **Score**

1	2	3	4	5

A.
$$10 - 5 \qquad 9 - 6 \qquad 15 - 6 \qquad 7 - 2 \qquad 11 - 5 \qquad 3 - 2 \qquad 13 - 7 \qquad 6 - 6 \qquad 12 - 3 \qquad 14 - 7$$

B.
$$4 - 3 \qquad 13 - 4 \qquad 5 - 2 \qquad 10 - 6 \qquad 6 - 4 \qquad 18 - 9 \qquad 8 - 8 \qquad 9 - 7 \qquad 12 - 8 \qquad 9 - 1$$

C.
$$8 - 3 \qquad 12 - 4 \qquad 17 - 9 \qquad 5 - 5 \qquad 13 - 8 \qquad 7 - 3 \qquad 10 - 3 \qquad 11 - 2 \qquad 15 - 7 \qquad 6 - 2$$

D.
$$14 - 6 \qquad 9 - 0 \qquad 7 - 7 \qquad 11 - 8 \qquad 2 - 0 \qquad 9 - 2 \qquad 14 - 8 \qquad 4 - 1 \qquad 8 - 4 \qquad 12 - 5$$

E.
$$4 - 4 \qquad 16 - 7 \qquad 6 - 5 \qquad 10 - 9 \qquad 12 - 9 \qquad 9 - 8 \qquad 1 - 0 \qquad 13 - 9 \qquad 5 - 0 \qquad 16 - 8$$

F.
$$9 - 5 \qquad 10 - 4 \qquad 11 - 7 \qquad 15 - 8 \qquad 5 - 3 \qquad 11 - 3 \qquad 13 - 5 \qquad 8 - 1 \qquad 9 - 9 \qquad 7 - 0$$

G.
$$14 - 9 \qquad 7 - 4 \qquad 6 - 0 \qquad 12 - 6 \qquad 3 - 3 \qquad 9 - 3 \qquad 17 - 8 \qquad 2 - 1 \qquad 10 - 7 \qquad 11 - 6$$

H.
$$8 - 0 \qquad 13 - 6 \qquad 7 - 1 \qquad 8 - 7 \qquad 3 - 1 \qquad 14 - 5 \qquad 7 - 5 \qquad 1 - 1 \qquad 10 - 1 \qquad 3 - 0$$

I.
$$8 - 6 \qquad 16 - 9 \qquad 2 - 2 \qquad 4 - 2 \qquad 10 - 8 \qquad 8 - 2 \qquad 5 - 4 \qquad 11 - 9 \qquad 0 - 0 \qquad 6 - 1$$

J.
$$11 - 4 \qquad 4 - 0 \qquad 9 - 4 \qquad 5 - 1 \qquad 12 - 7 \qquad 6 - 3 \qquad 10 - 2 \qquad 8 - 5 \qquad 15 - 9 \qquad 7 - 6$$

Minutes					Score
1	2	3	4	5	

A.
8	4	16	7	9	13	10	5	7	2
− 1	− 2	− 7	− 1	− 3	− 4	− 2	− 4	− 7	− 2

B.
9	5	10	13	6	1	9	14	11	9
− 8	− 5	− 7	− 8	− 4	− 0	− 0	− 9	− 6	− 1

C.
12	8	0	13	7	12	8	4	11	6
− 9	− 0	− 0	− 6	− 6	− 4	− 5	− 1	− 9	− 1

D.
5	14	8	10	3	12	7	10	2	9
− 0	− 6	− 8	− 3	− 0	− 7	− 0	− 1	− 1	− 7

E.
11	6	9	4	10	5	15	4	10	8
− 7	− 0	− 4	− 0	− 6	− 3	− 8	− 4	− 9	− 4

F.
7	2	12	6	9	11	8	14	7	12
− 5	− 0	− 3	− 3	− 2	− 5	− 3	− 5	− 3	− 6

G.
10	6	14	11	3	13	9	1	16	11
− 8	− 6	− 8	− 2	− 2	− 5	− 6	− 1	− 9	− 3

H.
4	13	7	15	10	18	6	17	11	5
− 3	− 7	− 2	− 6	− 5	− 9	− 2	− 8	− 8	− 1

I.
16	8	10	15	5	8	13	9	14	12
− 8	− 2	− 4	− 9	− 2	− 6	− 9	− 9	− 7	− 8

J.
3	15	9	6	17	7	11	3	12	8
− 1	− 7	− 5	− 5	− 9	− 4	− 4	− 3	− 5	− 7

Minutes

1	2	3	4	5

Score

Name_____

A.
$$\begin{array}{r} 2 \\ -\ 0 \end{array} \quad \begin{array}{r} 17 \\ -\ 8 \end{array} \quad \begin{array}{r} 9 \\ -\ 8 \end{array} \quad \begin{array}{r} 7 \\ -\ 0 \end{array} \quad \begin{array}{r} 16 \\ -\ 9 \end{array} \quad \begin{array}{r} 10 \\ -\ 6 \end{array} \quad \begin{array}{r} 4 \\ -\ 4 \end{array} \quad \begin{array}{r} 12 \\ -\ 6 \end{array} \quad \begin{array}{r} 8 \\ -\ 6 \end{array} \quad \begin{array}{r} 6 \\ -\ 2 \end{array}$$

B.
$$\begin{array}{r} 9 \\ -\ 1 \end{array} \quad \begin{array}{r} 5 \\ -\ 4 \end{array} \quad \begin{array}{r} 8 \\ -\ 2 \end{array} \quad \begin{array}{r} 1 \\ -\ 1 \end{array} \quad \begin{array}{r} 11 \\ -\ 5 \end{array} \quad \begin{array}{r} 6 \\ -\ 6 \end{array} \quad \begin{array}{r} 13 \\ -\ 4 \end{array} \quad \begin{array}{r} 7 \\ -\ 7 \end{array} \quad \begin{array}{r} 3 \\ -\ 0 \end{array} \quad \begin{array}{r} 9 \\ -\ 4 \end{array}$$

C.
$$\begin{array}{r} 11 \\ -\ 7 \end{array} \quad \begin{array}{r} 18 \\ -\ 9 \end{array} \quad \begin{array}{r} 6 \\ -\ 1 \end{array} \quad \begin{array}{r} 14 \\ -\ 5 \end{array} \quad \begin{array}{r} 7 \\ -\ 2 \end{array} \quad \begin{array}{r} 4 \\ -\ 0 \end{array} \quad \begin{array}{r} 17 \\ -\ 9 \end{array} \quad \begin{array}{r} 10 \\ -\ 1 \end{array} \quad \begin{array}{r} 9 \\ -\ 7 \end{array} \quad \begin{array}{r} 5 \\ -\ 1 \end{array}$$

D.
$$\begin{array}{r} 5 \\ -\ 0 \end{array} \quad \begin{array}{r} 10 \\ -\ 2 \end{array} \quad \begin{array}{r} 4 \\ -\ 2 \end{array} \quad \begin{array}{r} 10 \\ -\ 5 \end{array} \quad \begin{array}{r} 9 \\ -\ 0 \end{array} \quad \begin{array}{r} 5 \\ -\ 3 \end{array} \quad \begin{array}{r} 9 \\ -\ 3 \end{array} \quad \begin{array}{r} 8 \\ -\ 8 \end{array} \quad \begin{array}{r} 7 \\ -\ 4 \end{array} \quad \begin{array}{r} 11 \\ -\ 9 \end{array}$$

E.
$$\begin{array}{r} 8 \\ -\ 3 \end{array} \quad \begin{array}{r} 3 \\ -\ 1 \end{array} \quad \begin{array}{r} 10 \\ -\ 7 \end{array} \quad \begin{array}{r} 9 \\ -\ 6 \end{array} \quad \begin{array}{r} 6 \\ -\ 5 \end{array} \quad \begin{array}{r} 13 \\ -\ 6 \end{array} \quad \begin{array}{r} 12 \\ -\ 5 \end{array} \quad \begin{array}{r} 1 \\ -\ 0 \end{array} \quad \begin{array}{r} 12 \\ -\ 9 \end{array} \quad \begin{array}{r} 11 \\ -\ 2 \end{array}$$

F.
$$\begin{array}{r} 9 \\ -\ 9 \end{array} \quad \begin{array}{r} 8 \\ -\ 7 \end{array} \quad \begin{array}{r} 7 \\ -\ 6 \end{array} \quad \begin{array}{r} 11 \\ -\ 4 \end{array} \quad \begin{array}{r} 13 \\ -\ 8 \end{array} \quad \begin{array}{r} 8 \\ -\ 5 \end{array} \quad \begin{array}{r} 3 \\ -\ 3 \end{array} \quad \begin{array}{r} 15 \\ -\ 6 \end{array} \quad \begin{array}{r} 8 \\ -\ 1 \end{array} \quad \begin{array}{r} 2 \\ -\ 2 \end{array}$$

G.
$$\begin{array}{r} 7 \\ -\ 1 \end{array} \quad \begin{array}{r} 9 \\ -\ 2 \end{array} \quad \begin{array}{r} 14 \\ -\ 7 \end{array} \quad \begin{array}{r} 0 \\ -\ 0 \end{array} \quad \begin{array}{r} 12 \\ -\ 8 \end{array} \quad \begin{array}{r} 10 \\ -\ 4 \end{array} \quad \begin{array}{r} 6 \\ -\ 0 \end{array} \quad \begin{array}{r} 11 \\ -\ 8 \end{array} \quad \begin{array}{r} 10 \\ -\ 9 \end{array} \quad \begin{array}{r} 6 \\ -\ 4 \end{array}$$

H.
$$\begin{array}{r} 11 \\ -\ 6 \end{array} \quad \begin{array}{r} 7 \\ -\ 5 \end{array} \quad \begin{array}{r} 5 \\ -\ 2 \end{array} \quad \begin{array}{r} 13 \\ -\ 7 \end{array} \quad \begin{array}{r} 16 \\ -\ 8 \end{array} \quad \begin{array}{r} 8 \\ -\ 0 \end{array} \quad \begin{array}{r} 15 \\ -\ 8 \end{array} \quad \begin{array}{r} 4 \\ -\ 3 \end{array} \quad \begin{array}{r} 14 \\ -\ 9 \end{array} \quad \begin{array}{r} 12 \\ -\ 3 \end{array}$$

I.
$$\begin{array}{r} 3 \\ -\ 2 \end{array} \quad \begin{array}{r} 15 \\ -\ 9 \end{array} \quad \begin{array}{r} 12 \\ -\ 4 \end{array} \quad \begin{array}{r} 15 \\ -\ 7 \end{array} \quad \begin{array}{r} 7 \\ -\ 3 \end{array} \quad \begin{array}{r} 2 \\ -\ 1 \end{array} \quad \begin{array}{r} 16 \\ -\ 7 \end{array} \quad \begin{array}{r} 13 \\ -\ 9 \end{array} \quad \begin{array}{r} 14 \\ -\ 6 \end{array} \quad \begin{array}{r} 10 \\ -\ 8 \end{array}$$

J.
$$\begin{array}{r} 10 \\ -\ 3 \end{array} \quad \begin{array}{r} 5 \\ -\ 5 \end{array} \quad \begin{array}{r} 12 \\ -\ 7 \end{array} \quad \begin{array}{r} 8 \\ -\ 4 \end{array} \quad \begin{array}{r} 4 \\ -\ 1 \end{array} \quad \begin{array}{r} 11 \\ -\ 3 \end{array} \quad \begin{array}{r} 9 \\ -\ 5 \end{array} \quad \begin{array}{r} 14 \\ -\ 8 \end{array} \quad \begin{array}{r} 6 \\ -\ 3 \end{array} \quad \begin{array}{r} 13 \\ -\ 5 \end{array}$$

Minutes

1	2	3	4	5

Score

Name_____

A.
8	11	9	5	10	13	9	2	12	4
− 3	− 8	− 5	− 1	− 2	− 7	− 0	− 2	− 8	− 0

B.
13	3	18	6	15	5	12	8	10	7
− 4	− 2	− 9	− 5	− 8	− 5	− 6	− 0	− 4	− 4

C.
14	10	7	11	1	8	8	6	16	2
− 8	− 8	− 7	− 7	− 0	− 8	− 5	− 1	− 8	− 0

D.
6	12	4	11	5	10	9	11	3	5
− 6	− 9	− 2	− 3	− 0	− 1	− 4	− 5	− 3	− 3

E.
8	2	9	7	13	3	12	7	8	10
− 4	− 1	− 6	− 3	− 6	− 1	− 5	− 0	− 2	− 6

F.
5	10	6	12	9	16	6	15	0	14
− 2	− 3	− 0	− 3	− 9	− 7	− 3	− 6	− 0	− 5

G.
9	7	10	16	4	13	8	4	11	9
− 1	− 6	− 7	− 9	− 4	− 9	− 7	− 1	− 2	− 3

H.
11	1	14	9	15	7	14	13	8	17
− 9	− 1	− 7	− 8	− 9	− 2	− 9	− 5	− 1	− 8

I.
9	7	12	6	11	10	7	14	5	15
− 7	− 1	− 7	− 4	− 6	− 5	− 5	− 6	− 4	− 7

J.
11	4	8	13	6	17	3	10	9	12
− 4	− 3	− 6	− 8	− 2	− 9	− 0	− 9	− 2	− 4

Minutes

1	2	3	4	5

Score

A.
$$\begin{array}{r}12\\-\ 8\\\hline\end{array}\quad\begin{array}{r}4\\-\ 3\\\hline\end{array}\quad\begin{array}{r}17\\-\ 8\\\hline\end{array}\quad\begin{array}{r}12\\-\ 4\\\hline\end{array}\quad\begin{array}{r}3\\-\ 1\\\hline\end{array}\quad\begin{array}{r}13\\-\ 8\\\hline\end{array}\quad\begin{array}{r}10\\-\ 4\\\hline\end{array}\quad\begin{array}{r}8\\-\ 0\\\hline\end{array}\quad\begin{array}{r}11\\-\ 7\\\hline\end{array}\quad\begin{array}{r}6\\-\ 3\\\hline\end{array}$$

B.
$$\begin{array}{r}10\\-\ 6\\\hline\end{array}\quad\begin{array}{r}9\\-\ 1\\\hline\end{array}\quad\begin{array}{r}6\\-\ 2\\\hline\end{array}\quad\begin{array}{r}13\\-\ 6\\\hline\end{array}\quad\begin{array}{r}5\\-\ 4\\\hline\end{array}\quad\begin{array}{r}11\\-\ 6\\\hline\end{array}\quad\begin{array}{r}4\\-\ 2\\\hline\end{array}\quad\begin{array}{r}10\\-\ 2\\\hline\end{array}\quad\begin{array}{r}2\\-\ 0\\\hline\end{array}\quad\begin{array}{r}15\\-\ 7\\\hline\end{array}$$

C.
$$\begin{array}{r}11\\-\ 3\\\hline\end{array}\quad\begin{array}{r}1\\-\ 1\\\hline\end{array}\quad\begin{array}{r}15\\-\ 8\\\hline\end{array}\quad\begin{array}{r}8\\-\ 5\\\hline\end{array}\quad\begin{array}{r}7\\-\ 0\\\hline\end{array}\quad\begin{array}{r}16\\-\ 8\\\hline\end{array}\quad\begin{array}{r}5\\-\ 0\\\hline\end{array}\quad\begin{array}{r}14\\-\ 8\\\hline\end{array}\quad\begin{array}{r}9\\-\ 2\\\hline\end{array}\quad\begin{array}{r}7\\-\ 1\\\hline\end{array}$$

D.
$$\begin{array}{r}6\\-\ 6\\\hline\end{array}\quad\begin{array}{r}12\\-\ 7\\\hline\end{array}\quad\begin{array}{r}10\\-\ 5\\\hline\end{array}\quad\begin{array}{r}4\\-\ 1\\\hline\end{array}\quad\begin{array}{r}8\\-\ 4\\\hline\end{array}\quad\begin{array}{r}6\\-\ 1\\\hline\end{array}\quad\begin{array}{r}11\\-\ 4\\\hline\end{array}\quad\begin{array}{r}9\\-\ 9\\\hline\end{array}\quad\begin{array}{r}3\\-\ 0\\\hline\end{array}\quad\begin{array}{r}13\\-\ 4\\\hline\end{array}$$

E.
$$\begin{array}{r}7\\-\ 7\\\hline\end{array}\quad\begin{array}{r}9\\-\ 8\\\hline\end{array}\quad\begin{array}{r}4\\-\ 4\\\hline\end{array}\quad\begin{array}{r}14\\-\ 6\\\hline\end{array}\quad\begin{array}{r}6\\-\ 5\\\hline\end{array}\quad\begin{array}{r}11\\-\ 2\\\hline\end{array}\quad\begin{array}{r}1\\-\ 0\\\hline\end{array}\quad\begin{array}{r}12\\-\ 3\\\hline\end{array}\quad\begin{array}{r}9\\-\ 7\\\hline\end{array}\quad\begin{array}{r}8\\-\ 3\\\hline\end{array}$$

F.
$$\begin{array}{r}2\\-\ 2\\\hline\end{array}\quad\begin{array}{r}9\\-\ 5\\\hline\end{array}\quad\begin{array}{r}8\\-\ 7\\\hline\end{array}\quad\begin{array}{r}10\\-\ 9\\\hline\end{array}\quad\begin{array}{r}5\\-\ 3\\\hline\end{array}\quad\begin{array}{r}15\\-\ 6\\\hline\end{array}\quad\begin{array}{r}8\\-\ 2\\\hline\end{array}\quad\begin{array}{r}12\\-\ 9\\\hline\end{array}\quad\begin{array}{r}3\\-\ 3\\\hline\end{array}\quad\begin{array}{r}7\\-\ 6\\\hline\end{array}$$

G.
$$\begin{array}{r}8\\-\ 6\\\hline\end{array}\quad\begin{array}{r}13\\-\ 5\\\hline\end{array}\quad\begin{array}{r}12\\-\ 6\\\hline\end{array}\quad\begin{array}{r}3\\-\ 2\\\hline\end{array}\quad\begin{array}{r}18\\-\ 9\\\hline\end{array}\quad\begin{array}{r}7\\-\ 3\\\hline\end{array}\quad\begin{array}{r}6\\-\ 4\\\hline\end{array}\quad\begin{array}{r}11\\-\ 9\\\hline\end{array}\quad\begin{array}{r}5\\-\ 2\\\hline\end{array}\quad\begin{array}{r}10\\-\ 3\\\hline\end{array}$$

H.
$$\begin{array}{r}10\\-\ 8\\\hline\end{array}\quad\begin{array}{r}6\\-\ 0\\\hline\end{array}\quad\begin{array}{r}11\\-\ 5\\\hline\end{array}\quad\begin{array}{r}0\\-\ 0\\\hline\end{array}\quad\begin{array}{r}13\\-\ 7\\\hline\end{array}\quad\begin{array}{r}9\\-\ 6\\\hline\end{array}\quad\begin{array}{r}5\\-\ 1\\\hline\end{array}\quad\begin{array}{r}16\\-\ 7\\\hline\end{array}\quad\begin{array}{r}9\\-\ 3\\\hline\end{array}\quad\begin{array}{r}14\\-\ 5\\\hline\end{array}$$

I.
$$\begin{array}{r}14\\-\ 9\\\hline\end{array}\quad\begin{array}{r}4\\-\ 0\\\hline\end{array}\quad\begin{array}{r}10\\-\ 7\\\hline\end{array}\quad\begin{array}{r}16\\-\ 9\\\hline\end{array}\quad\begin{array}{r}8\\-\ 1\\\hline\end{array}\quad\begin{array}{r}7\\-\ 2\\\hline\end{array}\quad\begin{array}{r}10\\-\ 1\\\hline\end{array}\quad\begin{array}{r}9\\-\ 0\\\hline\end{array}\quad\begin{array}{r}17\\-\ 9\\\hline\end{array}\quad\begin{array}{r}7\\-\ 5\\\hline\end{array}$$

J.
$$\begin{array}{r}5\\-\ 5\\\hline\end{array}\quad\begin{array}{r}14\\-\ 7\\\hline\end{array}\quad\begin{array}{r}9\\-\ 4\\\hline\end{array}\quad\begin{array}{r}7\\-\ 4\\\hline\end{array}\quad\begin{array}{r}13\\-\ 9\\\hline\end{array}\quad\begin{array}{r}8\\-\ 8\\\hline\end{array}\quad\begin{array}{r}15\\-\ 9\\\hline\end{array}\quad\begin{array}{r}11\\-\ 8\\\hline\end{array}\quad\begin{array}{r}2\\-\ 1\\\hline\end{array}\quad\begin{array}{r}12\\-\ 5\\\hline\end{array}$$

Minutes

1	2	3	4	5

Score

A.	9 − 4	12 − 6	0 − 0	15 − 8	7 − 6	8 − 7	6 − 3	13 − 9	11 − 4	4 − 3
B.	11 − 7	2 − 2	8 − 2	10 − 3	4 − 2	14 − 6	12 − 5	4 − 0	9 − 7	7 − 1
C.	5 − 1	11 − 5	8 − 6	7 − 0	10 − 7	9 − 6	5 − 5	13 − 7	1 − 1	8 − 1
D.	10 − 4	7 − 5	13 − 5	3 − 0	14 − 8	7 − 2	10 − 2	5 − 0	17 − 9	8 − 5
E.	6 − 0	4 − 1	12 − 4	16 − 8	9 − 2	7 − 4	17 − 8	8 − 0	2 − 1	10 − 9
F.	6 − 4	13 − 8	7 − 3	11 − 3	1 − 0	15 − 9	6 − 1	12 − 3	9 − 9	5 − 4
G.	14 − 7	3 − 2	15 − 7	9 − 1	12 − 8	10 − 6	4 − 4	13 − 4	6 − 6	9 − 0
H.	7 − 7	9 − 5	18 − 9	6 − 2	14 − 5	8 − 4	14 − 9	9 − 8	3 − 3	11 − 9
I.	11 − 2	16 − 9	2 − 0	11 − 6	10 − 8	16 − 7	5 − 3	10 − 1	8 − 8	12 − 9
J.	5 − 2	12 − 7	10 − 5	8 − 3	13 − 6	9 − 3	3 − 1	15 − 6	11 − 8	6 − 5

Minutes

1	2	3	4	5

Score

Name_____

A.
$$\begin{array}{r}10\\-1\\\hline\end{array}\quad\begin{array}{r}6\\-3\\\hline\end{array}\quad\begin{array}{r}1\\-1\\\hline\end{array}\quad\begin{array}{r}13\\-4\\\hline\end{array}\quad\begin{array}{r}8\\-2\\\hline\end{array}\quad\begin{array}{r}5\\-3\\\hline\end{array}\quad\begin{array}{r}11\\-5\\\hline\end{array}\quad\begin{array}{r}14\\-8\\\hline\end{array}\quad\begin{array}{r}9\\-6\\\hline\end{array}\quad\begin{array}{r}3\\-2\\\hline\end{array}$$

B.
$$\begin{array}{r}12\\-8\\\hline\end{array}\quad\begin{array}{r}4\\-1\\\hline\end{array}\quad\begin{array}{r}12\\-3\\\hline\end{array}\quad\begin{array}{r}10\\-5\\\hline\end{array}\quad\begin{array}{r}13\\-8\\\hline\end{array}\quad\begin{array}{r}7\\-0\\\hline\end{array}\quad\begin{array}{r}12\\-7\\\hline\end{array}\quad\begin{array}{r}2\\-1\\\hline\end{array}\quad\begin{array}{r}18\\-9\\\hline\end{array}\quad\begin{array}{r}9\\-1\\\hline\end{array}$$

C.
$$\begin{array}{r}7\\-4\\\hline\end{array}\quad\begin{array}{r}9\\-9\\\hline\end{array}\quad\begin{array}{r}6\\-2\\\hline\end{array}\quad\begin{array}{r}9\\-3\\\hline\end{array}\quad\begin{array}{r}3\\-1\\\hline\end{array}\quad\begin{array}{r}11\\-9\\\hline\end{array}\quad\begin{array}{r}8\\-6\\\hline\end{array}\quad\begin{array}{r}15\\-6\\\hline\end{array}\quad\begin{array}{r}5\\-2\\\hline\end{array}\quad\begin{array}{r}13\\-9\\\hline\end{array}$$

D.
$$\begin{array}{r}2\\-0\\\hline\end{array}\quad\begin{array}{r}9\\-2\\\hline\end{array}\quad\begin{array}{r}8\\-1\\\hline\end{array}\quad\begin{array}{r}16\\-8\\\hline\end{array}\quad\begin{array}{r}6\\-6\\\hline\end{array}\quad\begin{array}{r}4\\-0\\\hline\end{array}\quad\begin{array}{r}13\\-7\\\hline\end{array}\quad\begin{array}{r}11\\-4\\\hline\end{array}\quad\begin{array}{r}5\\-5\\\hline\end{array}\quad\begin{array}{r}7\\-6\\\hline\end{array}$$

E.
$$\begin{array}{r}10\\-7\\\hline\end{array}\quad\begin{array}{r}8\\-5\\\hline\end{array}\quad\begin{array}{r}5\\-0\\\hline\end{array}\quad\begin{array}{r}9\\-5\\\hline\end{array}\quad\begin{array}{r}14\\-5\\\hline\end{array}\quad\begin{array}{r}7\\-3\\\hline\end{array}\quad\begin{array}{r}1\\-0\\\hline\end{array}\quad\begin{array}{r}12\\-6\\\hline\end{array}\quad\begin{array}{r}10\\-4\\\hline\end{array}\quad\begin{array}{r}17\\-9\\\hline\end{array}$$

F.
$$\begin{array}{r}5\\-4\\\hline\end{array}\quad\begin{array}{r}12\\-9\\\hline\end{array}\quad\begin{array}{r}9\\-8\\\hline\end{array}\quad\begin{array}{r}6\\-5\\\hline\end{array}\quad\begin{array}{r}8\\-0\\\hline\end{array}\quad\begin{array}{r}4\\-3\\\hline\end{array}\quad\begin{array}{r}14\\-7\\\hline\end{array}\quad\begin{array}{r}11\\-8\\\hline\end{array}\quad\begin{array}{r}3\\-0\\\hline\end{array}\quad\begin{array}{r}6\\-1\\\hline\end{array}$$

G.
$$\begin{array}{r}8\\-3\\\hline\end{array}\quad\begin{array}{r}3\\-3\\\hline\end{array}\quad\begin{array}{r}14\\-9\\\hline\end{array}\quad\begin{array}{r}11\\-2\\\hline\end{array}\quad\begin{array}{r}9\\-0\\\hline\end{array}\quad\begin{array}{r}15\\-8\\\hline\end{array}\quad\begin{array}{r}7\\-2\\\hline\end{array}\quad\begin{array}{r}10\\-3\\\hline\end{array}\quad\begin{array}{r}8\\-4\\\hline\end{array}\quad\begin{array}{r}12\\-4\\\hline\end{array}$$

H.
$$\begin{array}{r}7\\-7\\\hline\end{array}\quad\begin{array}{r}10\\-6\\\hline\end{array}\quad\begin{array}{r}4\\-4\\\hline\end{array}\quad\begin{array}{r}11\\-6\\\hline\end{array}\quad\begin{array}{r}6\\-4\\\hline\end{array}\quad\begin{array}{r}10\\-9\\\hline\end{array}\quad\begin{array}{r}16\\-7\\\hline\end{array}\quad\begin{array}{r}6\\-0\\\hline\end{array}\quad\begin{array}{r}16\\-9\\\hline\end{array}\quad\begin{array}{r}7\\-5\\\hline\end{array}$$

I.
$$\begin{array}{r}0\\-0\\\hline\end{array}\quad\begin{array}{r}14\\-6\\\hline\end{array}\quad\begin{array}{r}11\\-3\\\hline\end{array}\quad\begin{array}{r}12\\-5\\\hline\end{array}\quad\begin{array}{r}17\\-8\\\hline\end{array}\quad\begin{array}{r}9\\-7\\\hline\end{array}\quad\begin{array}{r}15\\-7\\\hline\end{array}\quad\begin{array}{r}13\\-6\\\hline\end{array}\quad\begin{array}{r}8\\-8\\\hline\end{array}\quad\begin{array}{r}15\\-9\\\hline\end{array}$$

J.
$$\begin{array}{r}7\\-1\\\hline\end{array}\quad\begin{array}{r}10\\-2\\\hline\end{array}\quad\begin{array}{r}5\\-1\\\hline\end{array}\quad\begin{array}{r}9\\-4\\\hline\end{array}\quad\begin{array}{r}4\\-2\\\hline\end{array}\quad\begin{array}{r}13\\-5\\\hline\end{array}\quad\begin{array}{r}8\\-7\\\hline\end{array}\quad\begin{array}{r}11\\-7\\\hline\end{array}\quad\begin{array}{r}2\\-2\\\hline\end{array}\quad\begin{array}{r}10\\-8\\\hline\end{array}$$

Minutes

1	2	3	4	5

Score

A. 10   9   4   13   2   15   7   11   8   6
   – 9   – 6   – 3   – 7   – 0   – 8   – 7   – 8   – 6   – 3

B.   6   10   12   3   17   10   4   13   9   7
   – 6   – 6   – 4   – 0   – 9   – 3   – 1   – 9   – 2   – 4

C.   8   13   6   10   5   16   8   14   1   9
   – 2   – 8   – 0   – 8   – 1   – 9   – 8   – 5   – 0   – 7

D.   4   16   7   13   5   12   10   8   3   10
   – 0   – 7   – 6   – 4   – 5   – 3   – 2   – 5   – 2   – 7

E. 12   1   10   9   7   15   9   5   14   6
   – 7   – 1   – 1   – 8   – 3   – 7   – 1   – 0   – 7   – 2

F.   9   6   11   4   18   8   2   14   7   11
   – 5   – 4   – 9   – 4   – 9   – 4   – 2   – 9   – 2   – 5

G.   6   11   8   13   3   17   10   7   12   5
   – 1   – 6   – 7   – 6   – 3   – 8   – 5   – 5   – 6   – 2

H.   8   2   15   9   11   5   14   12   6   11
   – 0   – 1   – 9   – 3   – 4   – 3   – 6   – 9   – 5   – 7

I.   9   7   14   5   12   9   8   16   3   11
   – 0   – 1   – 8   – 4   – 8   – 9   – 3   – 8   – 1   – 3

J.   4   15   9   7   12   11   0   10   13   8
   – 2   – 6   – 4   – 0   – 5   – 2   – 0   – 4   – 5   – 1

Minutes

1	2	3	4	5

Score

A.	11 − 9 =	10 − 5 =	3 − 3 =	9 − 8 =	7 − 1 =
B.	6 − 1 =	7 − 6 =	13 − 9 =	5 − 5 =	10 − 2 =
C.	12 − 8 =	2 − 1 =	5 − 0 =	13 − 5 =	11 − 5 =
D.	9 − 7 =	15 − 9 =	12 − 6 =	9 − 3 =	3 − 2 =
E.	4 − 1 =	6 − 4 =	11 − 4 =	1 − 0 =	8 − 3 =
F.	11 − 2 =	11 − 8 =	8 − 2 =	13 − 8 =	14 − 6 =
G.	16 − 9 =	10 − 8 =	15 − 7 =	7 − 5 =	9 − 6 =
H.	7 − 2 =	0 − 0 =	6 − 3 =	12 − 4 =	5 − 3 =
I.	5 − 4 =	17 − 9 =	9 − 2 =	10 − 4 =	8 − 1 =
J.	10 − 1 =	4 − 4 =	13 − 4 =	3 − 1 =	10 − 7 =
K.	13 − 6 =	8 − 7 =	6 − 6 =	11 − 7 =	4 − 3 =
L.	2 − 2 =	9 − 5 =	18 − 9 =	7 − 0 =	11 − 3 =
M.	12 − 5 =	14 − 5 =	8 − 5 =	9 − 0 =	2 − 0 =
N.	7 − 4 =	4 − 0 =	16 − 7 =	15 − 6 =	9 − 9 =
O.	10 − 6 =	17 − 8 =	1 − 1 =	5 − 2 =	12 − 9 =
P.	8 − 4 =	9 − 1 =	10 − 3 =	12 − 7 =	8 − 6 =
Q.	14 − 8 =	6 − 0 =	15 − 8 =	13 − 7 =	6 − 2 =
R.	6 − 5 =	11 − 6 =	8 − 0 =	8 − 8 =	16 − 8 =
S.	3 − 0 =	12 − 3 =	7 − 3 =	14 − 7 =	7 − 7 =
T.	9 − 4 =	5 − 1 =	10 − 9 =	4 − 2 =	14 − 9 =

Minutes

1	2	3	4	5

Score

Name_____

A. 11 – 5 =	13 – 4 =	10 – 8 =	10 – 5 =	1 – 1 =
B. 7 – 2 =	2 – 0 =	8 – 3 =	4 – 0 =	6 – 4 =
C. 13 – 7 =	10 – 3 =	15 – 9 =	12 – 4 =	11 – 8 =
D. 6 – 5 =	9 – 6 =	5 – 3 =	7 – 4 =	4 – 3 =
E. 14 – 6 =	11 – 4 =	17 – 8 =	12 – 7 =	3 – 1 =
F. 3 – 3 =	6 – 0 =	9 – 1 =	0 – 0 =	8 – 5 =
G. 15 – 7 =	12 – 3 =	10 – 7 =	9 – 8 =	12 – 9 =
H. 9 – 3 =	8 – 6 =	3 – 0 =	7 – 1 =	5 – 5 =
I. 11 – 9 =	16 – 9 =	14 – 5 =	13 – 6 =	11 – 3 =
J. 1 – 0 =	7 – 3 =	5 – 2 =	4 – 2 =	7 – 6 =
K. 12 – 8 =	11 – 2 =	15 – 6 =	10 – 4 =	12 – 6 =
L. 8 – 4 =	4 – 1 =	8 – 8 =	8 – 2 =	2 – 2 =
M. 9 – 7 =	10 – 2 =	14 – 8 =	17 – 9 =	16 – 8 =
N. 6 – 3 =	7 – 7 =	6 – 2 =	5 – 1 =	9 – 4 =
O. 13 – 5 =	16 – 7 =	13 – 9 =	10 – 1 =	14 – 7 =
P. 9 – 0 =	2 – 1 =	9 – 5 =	9 – 2 =	5 – 0 =
Q. 18 – 9 =	11 – 7 =	10 – 9 =	15 – 8 =	13 – 8 =
R. 5 – 4 =	6 – 1 =	7 – 0 =	4 – 4 =	8 – 7 =
S. 10 – 6 =	14 – 9 =	12 – 5 =	9 – 9 =	11 – 6 =
T. 8 – 1 =	7 – 5 =	3 – 2 =	8 – 0 =	6 – 6 =

Minutes

1	2	3	4	5

Score

A.	8 – 3 =	9 – 6 =	7 – 5 =	4 – 1 =	10 – 5 =
B.	13 – 6 =	5 – 2 =	14 – 7 =	12 – 7 =	6 – 3 =
C.	11 – 2 =	7 – 1 =	8 – 7 =	8 – 1 =	1 – 0 =
D.	2 – 2 =	11 – 6 =	4 – 0 =	9 – 9 =	11 – 9 =
E.	12 – 3 =	8 – 2 =	6 – 2 =	13 – 4 =	7 – 0 =
F.	7 – 6 =	10 – 1 =	9 – 5 =	5 – 1 =	11 – 5 =
G.	15 – 7 =	2 – 1 =	10 – 7 =	7 – 4 =	2 – 0 =
H.	6 – 0 =	6 – 6 =	0 – 0 =	9 – 8 =	9 – 4 =
I.	16 – 7 =	15 – 9 =	9 – 2 =	11 – 8 =	12 – 5 =
J.	4 – 2 =	5 – 5 =	14 – 6 =	3 – 3 =	5 – 4 =
K.	9 – 1 =	3 – 2 =	10 – 4 =	8 – 6 =	4 – 3 =
L.	12 – 6 =	17 – 8 =	7 – 3 =	10 – 9 =	10 – 3 =
M.	8 – 0 =	13 – 5 =	11 – 3 =	7 – 7 =	13 – 9 =
N.	9 – 7 =	6 – 1 =	5 – 0 =	13 – 7 =	3 – 1 =
O.	11 – 7 =	7 – 2 =	18 – 9 =	14 – 8 =	9 – 0 =
P.	1 – 1 =	12 – 9 =	12 – 4 =	6 – 5 =	15 – 8 =
Q.	8 – 4 =	16 – 9 =	9 – 3 =	15 – 6 =	11 – 4 =
R.	10 – 6 =	4 – 4 =	16 – 8 =	3 – 0 =	12 – 8 =
S.	14 – 9 =	8 – 8 =	10 – 8 =	10 – 2 =	8 – 5 =
T.	5 – 3 =	14 – 5 =	6 – 4 =	13 – 8 =	17 – 9 =

Minutes   **Score**

1	2	3	4	5

A.
$$\begin{array}{r}13\\-4\\\hline\end{array}\quad\begin{array}{r}4\\-0\\\hline\end{array}\quad\begin{array}{r}8\\+2\\\hline\end{array}\quad\begin{array}{r}14\\-7\\\hline\end{array}\quad\begin{array}{r}1\\+8\\\hline\end{array}\quad\begin{array}{r}9\\+8\\\hline\end{array}\quad\begin{array}{r}5\\-2\\\hline\end{array}\quad\begin{array}{r}10\\-4\\\hline\end{array}\quad\begin{array}{r}8\\+5\\\hline\end{array}\quad\begin{array}{r}7\\+2\\\hline\end{array}$$

B.
$$\begin{array}{r}3\\+0\\\hline\end{array}\quad\begin{array}{r}14\\-8\\\hline\end{array}\quad\begin{array}{r}2\\+2\\\hline\end{array}\quad\begin{array}{r}5\\-0\\\hline\end{array}\quad\begin{array}{r}9\\-7\\\hline\end{array}\quad\begin{array}{r}6\\+0\\\hline\end{array}\quad\begin{array}{r}9\\+3\\\hline\end{array}\quad\begin{array}{r}11\\-3\\\hline\end{array}\quad\begin{array}{r}0\\+4\\\hline\end{array}\quad\begin{array}{r}7\\-7\\\hline\end{array}$$

C.
$$\begin{array}{r}6\\-3\\\hline\end{array}\quad\begin{array}{r}0\\+1\\\hline\end{array}\quad\begin{array}{r}6\\+9\\\hline\end{array}\quad\begin{array}{r}5\\-4\\\hline\end{array}\quad\begin{array}{r}11\\-2\\\hline\end{array}\quad\begin{array}{r}2\\+9\\\hline\end{array}\quad\begin{array}{r}5\\+5\\\hline\end{array}\quad\begin{array}{r}8\\-5\\\hline\end{array}\quad\begin{array}{r}15\\-7\\\hline\end{array}\quad\begin{array}{r}4\\+6\\\hline\end{array}$$

D.
$$\begin{array}{r}3\\-3\\\hline\end{array}\quad\begin{array}{r}3\\+8\\\hline\end{array}\quad\begin{array}{r}7\\-5\\\hline\end{array}\quad\begin{array}{r}14\\-5\\\hline\end{array}\quad\begin{array}{r}4\\+9\\\hline\end{array}\quad\begin{array}{r}0\\-0\\\hline\end{array}\quad\begin{array}{r}9\\-1\\\hline\end{array}\quad\begin{array}{r}2\\+4\\\hline\end{array}\quad\begin{array}{r}7\\+0\\\hline\end{array}\quad\begin{array}{r}11\\-6\\\hline\end{array}$$

E.
$$\begin{array}{r}8\\-2\\\hline\end{array}\quad\begin{array}{r}9\\+0\\\hline\end{array}\quad\begin{array}{r}4\\+1\\\hline\end{array}\quad\begin{array}{r}6\\-2\\\hline\end{array}\quad\begin{array}{r}0\\+8\\\hline\end{array}\quad\begin{array}{r}13\\-7\\\hline\end{array}\quad\begin{array}{r}12\\-8\\\hline\end{array}\quad\begin{array}{r}7\\+6\\\hline\end{array}\quad\begin{array}{r}8\\+8\\\hline\end{array}\quad\begin{array}{r}1\\+2\\\hline\end{array}$$

F.
$$\begin{array}{r}1\\+1\\\hline\end{array}\quad\begin{array}{r}2\\-0\\\hline\end{array}\quad\begin{array}{r}8\\+4\\\hline\end{array}\quad\begin{array}{r}9\\-4\\\hline\end{array}\quad\begin{array}{r}3\\+7\\\hline\end{array}\quad\begin{array}{r}4\\+5\\\hline\end{array}\quad\begin{array}{r}7\\-6\\\hline\end{array}\quad\begin{array}{r}6\\+3\\\hline\end{array}\quad\begin{array}{r}9\\+1\\\hline\end{array}\quad\begin{array}{r}1\\-0\\\hline\end{array}$$

G.
$$\begin{array}{r}8\\-0\\\hline\end{array}\quad\begin{array}{r}7\\+8\\\hline\end{array}\quad\begin{array}{r}2\\+3\\\hline\end{array}\quad\begin{array}{r}12\\-5\\\hline\end{array}\quad\begin{array}{r}5\\+7\\\hline\end{array}\quad\begin{array}{r}9\\-6\\\hline\end{array}\quad\begin{array}{r}0\\+2\\\hline\end{array}\quad\begin{array}{r}16\\-9\\\hline\end{array}\quad\begin{array}{r}8\\+6\\\hline\end{array}\quad\begin{array}{r}5\\+2\\\hline\end{array}$$

H.
$$\begin{array}{r}1\\+7\\\hline\end{array}\quad\begin{array}{r}10\\-8\\\hline\end{array}\quad\begin{array}{r}7\\-3\\\hline\end{array}\quad\begin{array}{r}6\\+1\\\hline\end{array}\quad\begin{array}{r}10\\-9\\\hline\end{array}\quad\begin{array}{r}12\\-6\\\hline\end{array}\quad\begin{array}{r}18\\-9\\\hline\end{array}\quad\begin{array}{r}3\\+1\\\hline\end{array}\quad\begin{array}{r}12\\-9\\\hline\end{array}\quad\begin{array}{r}5\\+3\\\hline\end{array}$$

I.
$$\begin{array}{r}6\\-1\\\hline\end{array}\quad\begin{array}{r}9\\-9\\\hline\end{array}\quad\begin{array}{r}0\\+5\\\hline\end{array}\quad\begin{array}{r}13\\-8\\\hline\end{array}\quad\begin{array}{r}6\\+5\\\hline\end{array}\quad\begin{array}{r}5\\+9\\\hline\end{array}\quad\begin{array}{r}4\\-3\\\hline\end{array}\quad\begin{array}{r}7\\+4\\\hline\end{array}\quad\begin{array}{r}6\\-6\\\hline\end{array}\quad\begin{array}{r}11\\-7\\\hline\end{array}$$

J.
$$\begin{array}{r}3\\+4\\\hline\end{array}\quad\begin{array}{r}15\\-6\\\hline\end{array}\quad\begin{array}{r}17\\-9\\\hline\end{array}\quad\begin{array}{r}9\\+7\\\hline\end{array}\quad\begin{array}{r}2\\+6\\\hline\end{array}\quad\begin{array}{r}3\\-1\\\hline\end{array}\quad\begin{array}{r}10\\-3\\\hline\end{array}\quad\begin{array}{r}1\\+5\\\hline\end{array}\quad\begin{array}{r}4\\+4\\\hline\end{array}\quad\begin{array}{r}8\\-1\\\hline\end{array}$$

Minutes

1	2	3	4	5

Score

Name _____

A.	8 + 1	17 − 8	2 + 2	12 − 7	1 + 8	3 + 2	8 − 3	4 + 6	11 − 7	8 + 9
B.	11 − 2	7 + 3	5 + 5	6 − 1	14 − 6	2 + 8	4 − 1	7 + 6	0 + 5	12 − 6
C.	9 + 5	0 + 2	1 − 1	4 − 0	6 + 3	9 − 7	5 + 8	15 − 8	6 + 0	9 − 5
D.	6 − 5	6 + 1	5 + 9	11 − 6	9 − 9	2 + 1	7 − 0	8 − 8	4 + 3	1 + 2
E.	7 + 2	6 − 2	3 + 0	1 + 9	12 − 4	3 + 3	9 + 3	8 − 7	7 − 2	2 + 6
F.	2 − 0	3 + 9	8 − 1	4 + 4	11 − 5	5 − 4	10 − 1	0 + 0	9 + 7	8 + 5
G.	1 + 6	13 − 9	1 − 0	7 + 4	8 + 7	2 + 4	18 − 9	4 + 1	6 + 9	11 − 9
H.	5 + 4	7 − 5	0 + 6	10 − 7	5 − 3	7 − 4	5 + 0	14 − 9	4 − 4	14 − 8
I.	9 + 0	7 + 7	8 − 2	3 − 3	4 + 8	10 − 2	11 − 8	10 − 4	0 + 7	9 − 6
J.	8 − 0	3 + 5	9 + 4	11 − 3	4 − 3	1 + 1	15 − 6	6 + 7	8 + 8	16 − 7

Minutes | 1 | 2 | 3 | 4 | 5 |

Score [ ]

Name_____   **Addition and Subtraction Facts: 0 to 18**

A.
8	6	7	3	13	15	9	5	1	8
− 8	+ 9	− 0	+ 3	− 9	− 6	+ 5	− 2	+ 6	− 1

B.
11	8	0	18	5	2	6	8	7	9
− 9	+ 5	+ 4	− 9	− 3	+ 2	+ 4	− 5	+ 3	+ 0

C.
5	14	9	7	5	8	0	3	5	7
+ 7	− 8	+ 7	+ 4	− 5	− 4	+ 2	− 2	+ 8	− 2

D.
9	3	12	3	8	1	9	8	15	2
− 4	+ 0	− 4	+ 4	− 6	+ 9	− 3	+ 0	− 7	+ 8

E.
1	12	3	4	2	11	2	5	8	13
+ 8	− 5	− 3	+ 2	− 0	− 6	+ 7	+ 0	+ 9	− 6

F.
7	0	15	8	6	4	9	0	4	0
− 3	+ 1	− 8	− 7	+ 2	+ 1	− 6	− 0	+ 8	+ 9

G.
6	11	8	6	9	4	2	3	11	7
+ 1	− 7	+ 1	− 4	+ 4	− 0	+ 1	+ 7	− 3	+ 7

H.
5	3	7	1	11	6	2	4	17	5
− 4	+ 8	+ 2	+ 0	− 5	+ 6	− 1	+ 6	− 8	+ 3

I.
2	12	7	9	5	0	10	14	6	13
+ 5	− 9	− 7	+ 3	+ 5	+ 6	− 1	− 9	− 5	− 7

J.
4	7	6	4	16	8	6	10	1	11
− 1	+ 9	− 1	+ 5	− 8	+ 6	− 0	− 2	+ 3	− 2

Minutes | 1 | 2 | 3 | 4 | 5 | **Score**

A.
$$\begin{array}{r} 13 \\ -5 \\ \hline \end{array} \quad \begin{array}{r} 7 \\ +1 \\ \hline \end{array} \quad \begin{array}{r} 6 \\ +4 \\ \hline \end{array} \quad \begin{array}{r} 16 \\ -7 \\ \hline \end{array} \quad \begin{array}{r} 12 \\ -7 \\ \hline \end{array} \quad \begin{array}{r} 4 \\ +7 \\ \hline \end{array} \quad \begin{array}{r} 2 \\ +9 \\ \hline \end{array} \quad \begin{array}{r} 7 \\ -1 \\ \hline \end{array} \quad \begin{array}{r} 6 \\ -2 \\ \hline \end{array} \quad \begin{array}{r} 0 \\ +3 \\ \hline \end{array}$$

B.
$$\begin{array}{r} 3 \\ +4 \\ \hline \end{array} \quad \begin{array}{r} 10 \\ -1 \\ \hline \end{array} \quad \begin{array}{r} 13 \\ -6 \\ \hline \end{array} \quad \begin{array}{r} 1 \\ +2 \\ \hline \end{array} \quad \begin{array}{r} 9 \\ -0 \\ \hline \end{array} \quad \begin{array}{r} 9 \\ +3 \\ \hline \end{array} \quad \begin{array}{r} 4 \\ -2 \\ \hline \end{array} \quad \begin{array}{r} 5 \\ +2 \\ \hline \end{array} \quad \begin{array}{r} 8 \\ +7 \\ \hline \end{array} \quad \begin{array}{r} 16 \\ -8 \\ \hline \end{array}$$

C.
$$\begin{array}{r} 2 \\ -1 \\ \hline \end{array} \quad \begin{array}{r} 7 \\ -3 \\ \hline \end{array} \quad \begin{array}{r} 8 \\ +1 \\ \hline \end{array} \quad \begin{array}{r} 10 \\ -2 \\ \hline \end{array} \quad \begin{array}{r} 0 \\ -0 \\ \hline \end{array} \quad \begin{array}{r} 5 \\ +3 \\ \hline \end{array} \quad \begin{array}{r} 14 \\ -5 \\ \hline \end{array} \quad \begin{array}{r} 0 \\ +2 \\ \hline \end{array} \quad \begin{array}{r} 3 \\ +6 \\ \hline \end{array} \quad \begin{array}{r} 8 \\ -2 \\ \hline \end{array}$$

D.
$$\begin{array}{r} 5 \\ -1 \\ \hline \end{array} \quad \begin{array}{r} 0 \\ +6 \\ \hline \end{array} \quad \begin{array}{r} 4 \\ +5 \\ \hline \end{array} \quad \begin{array}{r} 6 \\ -4 \\ \hline \end{array} \quad \begin{array}{r} 11 \\ -4 \\ \hline \end{array} \quad \begin{array}{r} 1 \\ +9 \\ \hline \end{array} \quad \begin{array}{r} 7 \\ +2 \\ \hline \end{array} \quad \begin{array}{r} 8 \\ -7 \\ \hline \end{array} \quad \begin{array}{r} 9 \\ -9 \\ \hline \end{array} \quad \begin{array}{r} 4 \\ +9 \\ \hline \end{array}$$

E.
$$\begin{array}{r} 5 \\ +5 \\ \hline \end{array} \quad \begin{array}{r} 11 \\ -6 \\ \hline \end{array} \quad \begin{array}{r} 7 \\ -6 \\ \hline \end{array} \quad \begin{array}{r} 2 \\ +0 \\ \hline \end{array} \quad \begin{array}{r} 6 \\ -3 \\ \hline \end{array} \quad \begin{array}{r} 6 \\ +9 \\ \hline \end{array} \quad \begin{array}{r} 3 \\ +5 \\ \hline \end{array} \quad \begin{array}{r} 12 \\ -9 \\ \hline \end{array} \quad \begin{array}{r} 10 \\ -6 \\ \hline \end{array} \quad \begin{array}{r} 6 \\ +0 \\ \hline \end{array}$$

F.
$$\begin{array}{r} 8 \\ -4 \\ \hline \end{array} \quad \begin{array}{r} 2 \\ +7 \\ \hline \end{array} \quad \begin{array}{r} 10 \\ -3 \\ \hline \end{array} \quad \begin{array}{r} 9 \\ +2 \\ \hline \end{array} \quad \begin{array}{r} 4 \\ -4 \\ \hline \end{array} \quad \begin{array}{r} 8 \\ +6 \\ \hline \end{array} \quad \begin{array}{r} 3 \\ -1 \\ \hline \end{array} \quad \begin{array}{r} 0 \\ +8 \\ \hline \end{array} \quad \begin{array}{r} 3 \\ +2 \\ \hline \end{array} \quad \begin{array}{r} 9 \\ -3 \\ \hline \end{array}$$

G.
$$\begin{array}{r} 7 \\ +0 \\ \hline \end{array} \quad \begin{array}{r} 4 \\ -1 \\ \hline \end{array} \quad \begin{array}{r} 6 \\ +7 \\ \hline \end{array} \quad \begin{array}{r} 0 \\ +1 \\ \hline \end{array} \quad \begin{array}{r} 2 \\ +3 \\ \hline \end{array} \quad \begin{array}{r} 5 \\ -0 \\ \hline \end{array} \quad \begin{array}{r} 8 \\ +3 \\ \hline \end{array} \quad \begin{array}{r} 6 \\ -5 \\ \hline \end{array} \quad \begin{array}{r} 7 \\ -7 \\ \hline \end{array} \quad \begin{array}{r} 12 \\ -5 \\ \hline \end{array}$$

H.
$$\begin{array}{r} 1 \\ +4 \\ \hline \end{array} \quad \begin{array}{r} 10 \\ -8 \\ \hline \end{array} \quad \begin{array}{r} 4 \\ -3 \\ \hline \end{array} \quad \begin{array}{r} 9 \\ +8 \\ \hline \end{array} \quad \begin{array}{r} 5 \\ +9 \\ \hline \end{array} \quad \begin{array}{r} 1 \\ +0 \\ \hline \end{array} \quad \begin{array}{r} 12 \\ -6 \\ \hline \end{array} \quad \begin{array}{r} 7 \\ +7 \\ \hline \end{array} \quad \begin{array}{r} 14 \\ -8 \\ \hline \end{array} \quad \begin{array}{r} 4 \\ +8 \\ \hline \end{array}$$

I.
$$\begin{array}{r} 3 \\ +0 \\ \hline \end{array} \quad \begin{array}{r} 5 \\ -5 \\ \hline \end{array} \quad \begin{array}{r} 4 \\ +0 \\ \hline \end{array} \quad \begin{array}{r} 5 \\ +1 \\ \hline \end{array} \quad \begin{array}{r} 9 \\ -4 \\ \hline \end{array} \quad \begin{array}{r} 8 \\ -6 \\ \hline \end{array} \quad \begin{array}{r} 9 \\ +4 \\ \hline \end{array} \quad \begin{array}{r} 2 \\ +5 \\ \hline \end{array} \quad \begin{array}{r} 18 \\ -9 \\ \hline \end{array} \quad \begin{array}{r} 10 \\ -7 \\ \hline \end{array}$$

J.
$$\begin{array}{r} 13 \\ -8 \\ \hline \end{array} \quad \begin{array}{r} 8 \\ +4 \\ \hline \end{array} \quad \begin{array}{r} 11 \\ -8 \\ \hline \end{array} \quad \begin{array}{r} 6 \\ +5 \\ \hline \end{array} \quad \begin{array}{r} 1 \\ +8 \\ \hline \end{array} \quad \begin{array}{r} 16 \\ -7 \\ \hline \end{array} \quad \begin{array}{r} 17 \\ -9 \\ \hline \end{array} \quad \begin{array}{r} 8 \\ -0 \\ \hline \end{array} \quad \begin{array}{r} 9 \\ +6 \\ \hline \end{array} \quad \begin{array}{r} 7 \\ +8 \\ \hline \end{array}$$

Minutes   **Score**

1	2	3	4	5

Name _____ Grade _____

★ ★ ★ SCORE SHEET ★ ★ ★

Page	Time	0–69	70	71	72	73	74	75	76	77	78	79	80	81	82	83	84	85	86	87	88	89	90	91	92	93	94	95	96	97	98	99	100

Math Master

This certificate is presented to

_____

for attaining 100% accuracy within a _____ minute time limit on the Minute Math Tests!

Fast Facts Award
presented to

_____

who has demonstrated the ability to think quickly and accurately when working _____ problems.

Date _____

Signature_____

Add to solve the problems.

A. 5 + 4 = ___

B. 9 + 3 = ___

C. 9 + 1 = ___

D. 8 + 0 = ___

E. 7 + 0 = ___

F. 4 + 8 = ___

G. 0 + 4 = ___

H. 9 + 9 = ___

I. 8 + 3 = ___

J. 7 + 6 = ___

K. 4 + 6 = ___

L. 2 + 5 = ___

M. 9 + 5 = ___

N. 1 + 9 = ___

O. 3 + 7 = ___

P. 5 + 8 = ___

Q. 6 + 3 = ___

R. 2 + 8 = ___

S. 7 + 9 = ___

Name_____

Add or subtract to solve the problems.

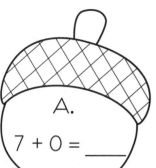

A.
7 + 0 = ___

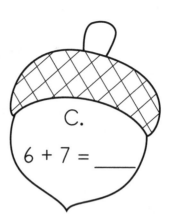

B.
15 − 6 = ___

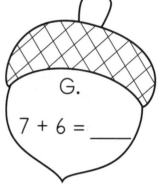

C.
6 + 7 = ___

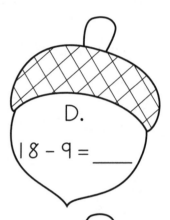

D.
18 − 9 = ___

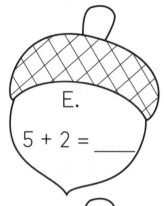

E.
5 + 2 = ___

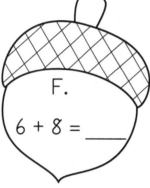

F.
6 + 8 = ___

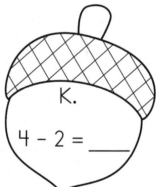

G.
7 + 6 = ___

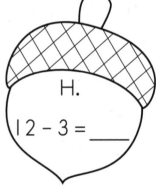

H.
12 − 3 = ___

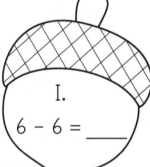

I.
6 − 6 = ___

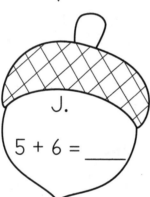

J.
5 + 6 = ___

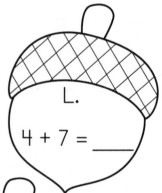

K.
4 − 2 = ___

L.
4 + 7 = ___

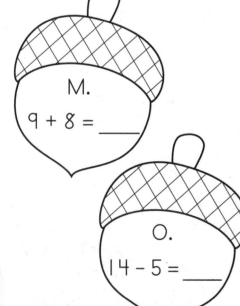

M.
9 + 8 = ___

N.
8 + 4 = ___

O.
14 − 5 = ___

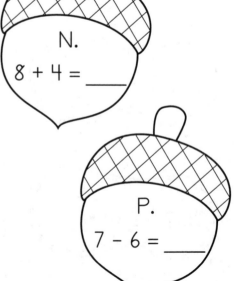

P.
7 − 6 = ___

Name_____

Add to solve the problems.

A.
   3
+ 7

B.
   6
+ 2

C.
   5
+ 8

D.
   7
+ 1

E.
   8
+ 7

F.
   9
+ 9

G.
   6
+ 7

H.
   8
+ 9

I.
   6
+ 8

J.
   4
+ 9

K.
   9
+ 4

L.
   0
+ 4

M.
   4
+ 5

N.
   6
+ 9

O.
   7
+ 7

P.
   5
+ 6

Q.
   2
+ 8

R.
   9
+ 7

S.
   8
+ 4

T.
   2
+ 9

U.
   9
+ 3

Subtract to solve the problems.

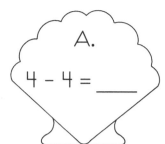
A.
4 – 4 = ____

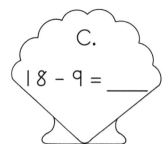
B.
1 – 0 = ____

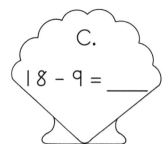
C.
18 – 9 = ____

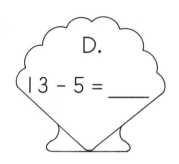
D.
13 – 5 = ____

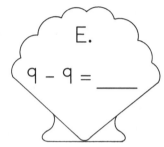
E.
9 – 9 = ____

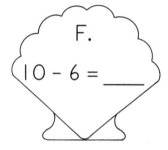
F.
10 – 6 = ____

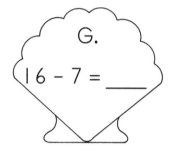
G.
16 – 7 = ____

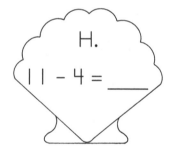
H.
11 – 4 = ____

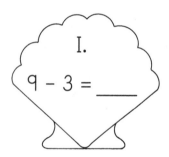
I.
9 – 3 = ____

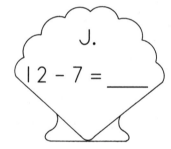
J.
12 – 7 = ____

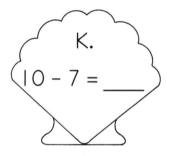
K.
10 – 7 = ____

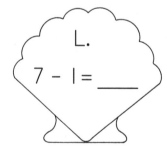
L.
7 – 1 = ____

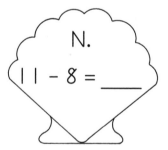
M.
14 – 8 = ____

N.
11 – 8 = ____

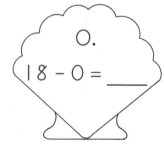
O.
18 – 0 = ____

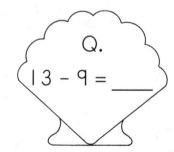
P.
12 – 6 = ____

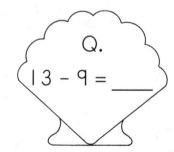
Q.
13 – 9 = ____

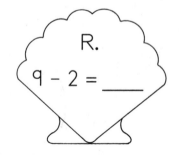
R.
9 – 2 = ____

Name_____

Add to solve the problems. Then, use the key to color the picture.

Key
10 = blue   12 = gray   18 = brown   6 = green   14 = yellow   8 = orange

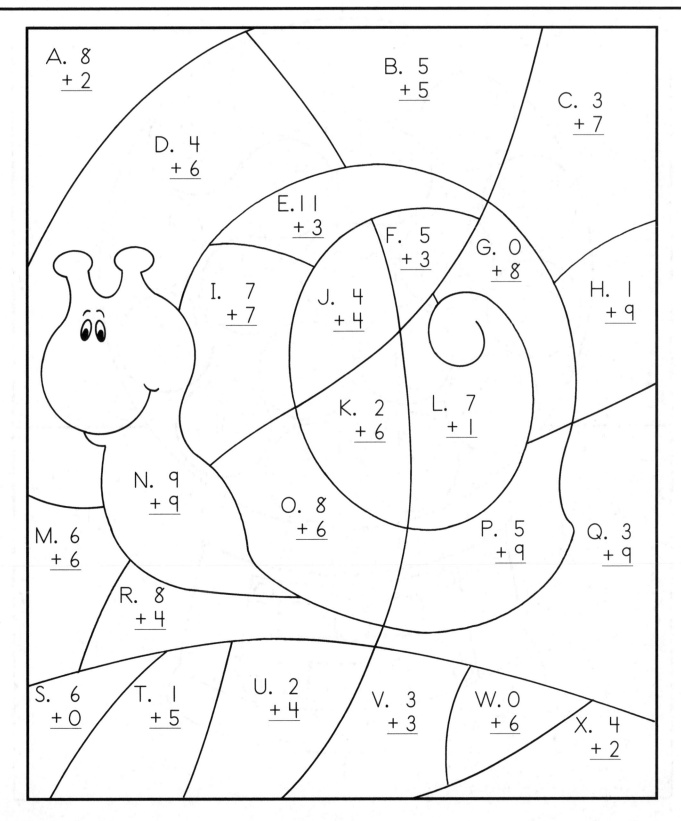

A. 8
  + 2

B. 5
  + 5

C. 3
  + 7

D. 4
  + 6

E. 11
  + 3

F. 5
  + 3

G. 0
  + 8

H. 1
  + 9

I. 7
  + 7

J. 4
  + 4

K. 2
  + 6

L. 7
  + 1

N. 9
  + 9

M. 6
  + 6

O. 8
  + 6

P. 5
  + 9

Q. 3
  + 9

R. 8
  + 4

S. 6
  + 0

T. 1
  + 5

U. 2
  + 4

V. 3
  + 3

W. 0
  + 6

X. 4
  + 2

Name_____

Subtract to solve tle problems. Then, use the key to color the picture.

Key
3 = blue   4 = purple   5 = green   7 = red   8 = orange   9 = yellow

A. 15 – 7 = ____

B. 17 – 9 = ____

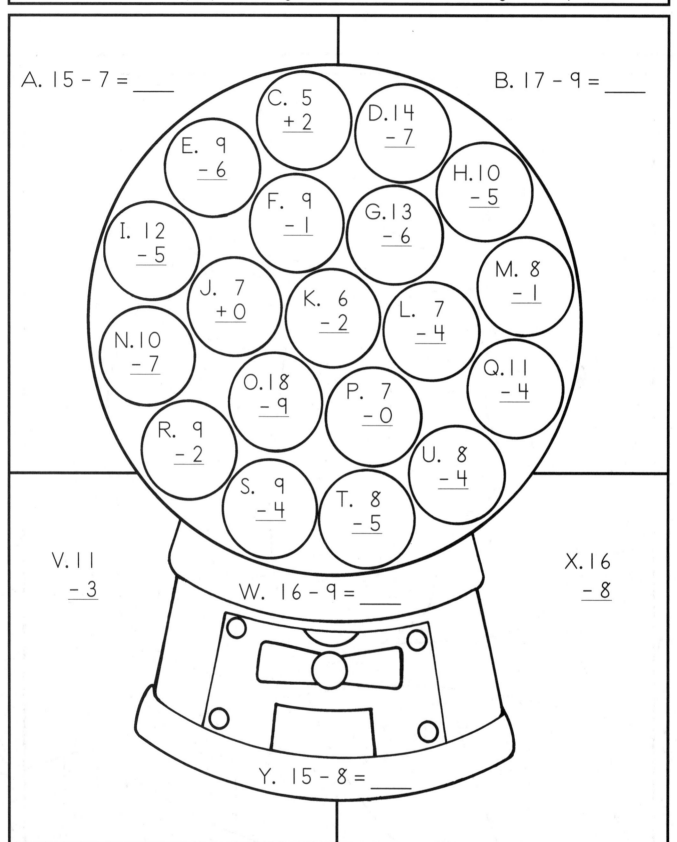

C. 5 + 2
D. 14 – 7
E. 9 – 6
H. 10 – 5
F. 9 – 1
G. 13 – 6
I. 12 – 5
M. 8 – 1
J. 7 + 0
K. 6 – 2
L. 7 – 4
N. 10 – 7
O. 18 – 9
P. 7 – 0
Q. 11 – 4
R. 9 – 2
U. 8 – 4
S. 9 – 4
T. 8 – 5

V. 11 – 3

W. 16 – 9 = ____

X. 16 – 8

Y. 15 – 8 = ____

34

Match the eggs with the correct hens.

A.
 6
+ 4

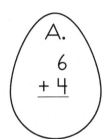

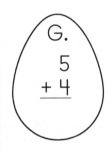

G.
 5
+ 4

B.
 6
+ 6

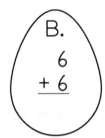

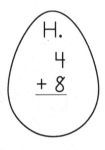

H.
 4
+ 8

C.
 4
+ 2

I.
 9
+ 9

D.
 0
+ 4

J.
 4
+ 3

E.
 6
+ 2

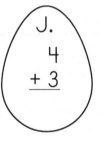

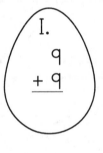

K.
 7
+ 8

F.
 8
+ 5

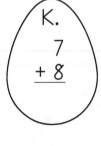

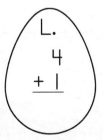

L.
 4
+ 1

Name_____

Help the cow find her way to the barn. Add to solve the problems.

A. 2 + 6 = ____   B. 3 + 2 = ____

E. 9 + 8 = ____   D. 3 + 9 = ____   C. 9 + 6 = ____

F. 6 + 3 = ____   G. 1 + 3 = ____   H. 8 + 5 = ____

K. 6 + 5 = ____   J. 7 + 9 = ____   I. 9 + 9 = ____

L. 6 + 8 = ____   M. 8 + 2 = ____

Name_____

Add to solve the problems in the problem list. Use + and = to find the same problems hidden across or down in the puzzle. Circle the hidden problems.

Problem List

7 + 4 = _____

4 + 9 = _____

7 + 7 = _____

8 + 4 = _____

9 + 9 = _____

6 + 8 = _____

8 + 7 = _____

9 + 7 = _____

3 + 9 = _____

8 + 8 = _____

3 + 8 = _____

1 + 8 = _____

6 + 7 = _____

3 + 7 = _____

9 + 6 = _____

7 + 5 = _____

5 + 5 = _____

5 + 8 = _____

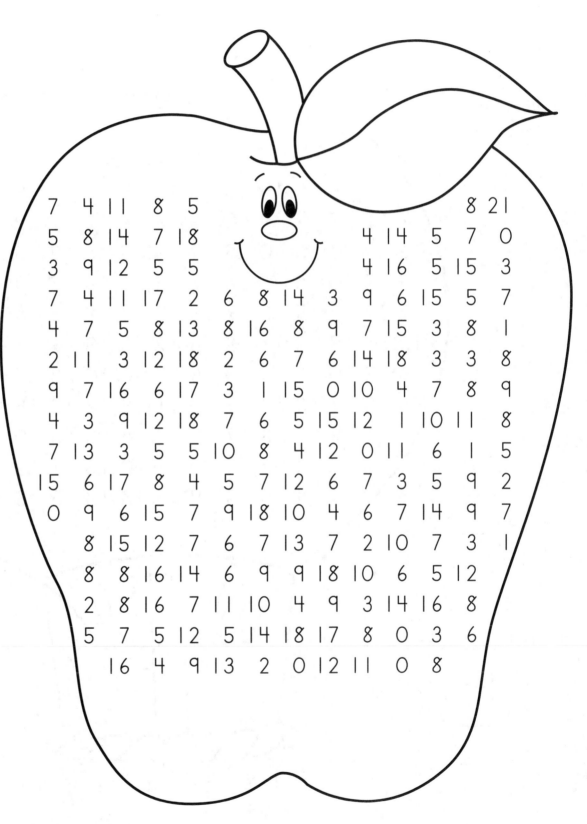

Subtract to solve the problems in the problem list. Use – and = to find the same problems hidden across or down in the puzzle. Circle the hidden problems.

Problem List

10 – 3 = _____

11 – 4 = _____

10 – 5 = _____

9 – 3 = _____

9 – 9 = _____

18 – 9 = _____

8 – 1 = _____

8 – 3 = _____

16 – 7 = _____

9 – 0 = _____

7 – 2 = _____

17 – 8 = _____

13 – 5 = _____

9 – 8 = _____

14 – 6 = _____

8 – 4 = _____

12 – 3 = _____

11 – 2 = _____

```
11 16  9 14  5  9 10  5  5  7  4 12
    2  7  9  9  0  9  8  6 12  7  2  5  8
16  9  8 13  0  9 12  1  8  6  9  3  6  8 13
 4  0 10  9  7 16  7  9  1 16  7  9 17  4  5
 7 11 12  4  8 17  8  9  7 18 13  8  8  4  9
13 18  9  9  1  8 16 12  3  9 18  1  9  8 12
 6  9 10  3  7  9  8  9  0 10  3  7 10  5 14
    9  7  3 18  1 10 11 14  7 13 15  9  1  6
   11  4  7  8  7  9  0  5  9  3  0  8  2  8
      17  4  3  3  0  6  0 16  1 12  1  4
      14  5  8  9  5 18 13  5  8  1
```

Name_____

Add to solve the problems.

A. 8
  + 5

B. 6
  + 9

C. 4
  + 8

D. 5
  + 5

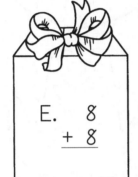

E. 8
  + 8

F. 9
  + 8

G. 6
  + 7

H. 1
  + 9

I. 9
  + 9

J. 7
  + 4

K. 4
  + 4

L. 8
  + 6

M. 0
  + 9

N. 7
  + 5

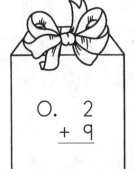

O. 2
  + 9

Name_____

Add or subtract to solve the problems.

A.   5
    + 6

B.   9
    + 3

C.   8
    + 8

D.   9
    + 5

E.   9
    + 9

F.   8
    + 9

G.   8
    + 6

H.   6
    + 2

I.   6
    + 7

J.   9
    + 4

K.   7
    - 7

L. 13
    - 8

M. 18
   - 9

N. 16
    - 7

O. 10
    - 1

P. 14
    - 9

Q. 15
    - 7

R. 12
    - 9

S. 10
    - 7

T.   8
    - 8

U. 14
    - 7

V. 16
    - 8

40

Add or subtract to solve the problems.

A. 7
  + 1

B. 16
  − 7

C. 12
  − 6

D. 10
  − 6

E. 8
  − 6

F. 9
  + 4

G. 18
  − 9

H. 7
  + 8

I. 7
  − 7

J. 14
  − 8

K. 15
  − 9

L. 1
  + 0

M. 4
  + 7

N. 3
  + 4

O. 8
  + 1

P. 6
  + 9

Q. 11
  − 4

R. 3
  + 5

S. 14
  − 5

T. 8
  + 6

U. 13
  − 5

V. 5
  + 9

W. 1
  + 2

X. 14
  − 7

Y. 15
  − 5

Z. 16
  − 8

AA. 4
  + 8

BB. 9
  + 1

CC. 12
  − 7

DD. 9
  − 3

EE. 9
  + 7

Add or subtract to solve the problems.

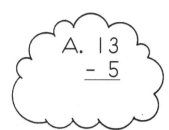
A. 13
  - 5

B. 4
  + 7

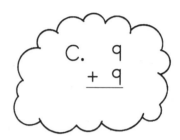
C. 9
  + 9

D. 2
 + 9

E. 6
 + 0

F. 6
 + 4

G. 7
 - 1

H. 12
  - 5

I. 16
 - 7

J. 4
 - 2

K. 14
 - 8

L. 12
 - 7

M. 8
 - 7

N. 9
 + 4

O. 5
 + 6

P. 12
 - 9

Q. 2
 + 5

R. 15
 - 5

S. 7
 + 6

Name_____   **Addition and Subtraction Facts: 0 to 18**

Add or subtract to solve the problems. Then, use the key to color the picture.

Key					
10 = green	6 = gray	14 = pink	9 = light blue	4 = yellow	12 = blue

A. $9 - 5$

B. $10 - 1$

G. $12 - 3$

C. $2 + 2$

E. $11 - 7$

D. $7 - 3$

F. $9 + 5$

J. $10 - 4$

H. $2 + 8$

I. $6 - 2$

K. $7 + 3$

L. $5 + 5$

M. $7 + 5$

N. $13 - 7$

O. $10 - 6$

P. $4 - 0$

Q. $7 - 1$

U. $12 - 8$

R. $7 + 2$

S. $6 + 6$

T. $9 + 3$

V. $8 + 4$ ___

W. $18 - 9$

X. $3 + 3 =$ ___

Z. $5 - 1$

Y. $3 + 1 =$ ___

43

Name_____

Add or subtract to solve the problems. Then, use the key to color the picture.

Key
14 = green   9 = orange   7 = pink   8 = light blue   13 = yellow

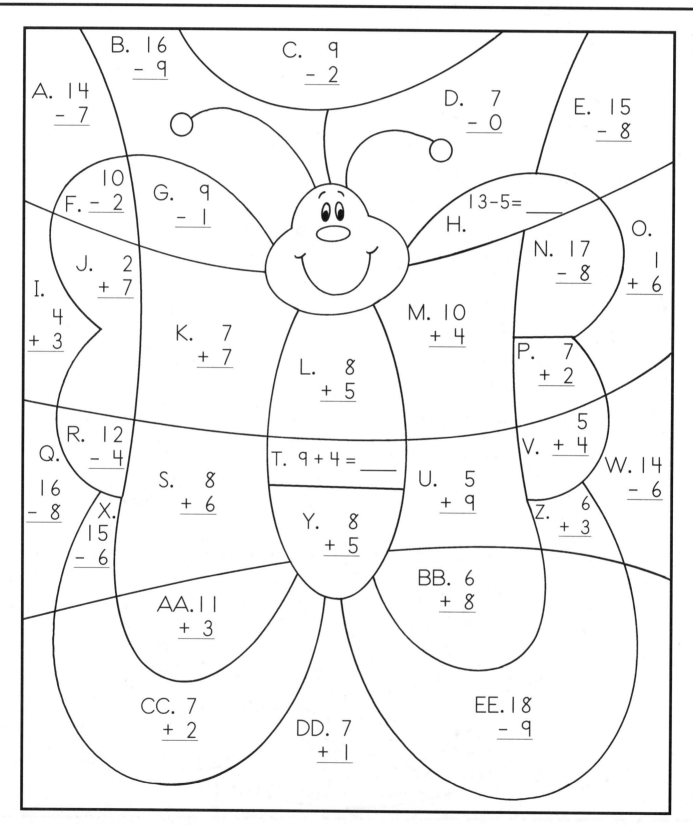

B. 16
－ 9

C. 9
－ 2

A. 14
－ 7

D. 7
－ 0

E. 15
－ 8

10
F. － 2

G. 9
－ 1

13－5= ___
H.

N. 17
－ 8

O.
1
＋ 6

J. 2
＋ 7

I.
4
＋ 3

K. 7
＋ 7

M. 10
＋ 4

L. 8
＋ 5

P. 7
＋ 2

5
V. ＋ 4

R. 12
－ 4

Q.
16
－ 8

T. 9 ＋ 4 = ___

S. 8
＋ 6

U. 5
＋ 9

W. 14
－ 6

X.
15
－ 6

Y. 8
＋ 5

Z. 6
＋ 3

AA. 11
＋ 3

BB. 6
＋ 8

CC. 7
＋ 2

DD. 7
＋ 1

EE. 18
－ 9

44

Name_____

Subtract to solve the problems. Then, use the key to color the picture.

Key
3 = black   4 = orange   5 = brown   6 = blue   7 = green   8 = red   9 = yellow

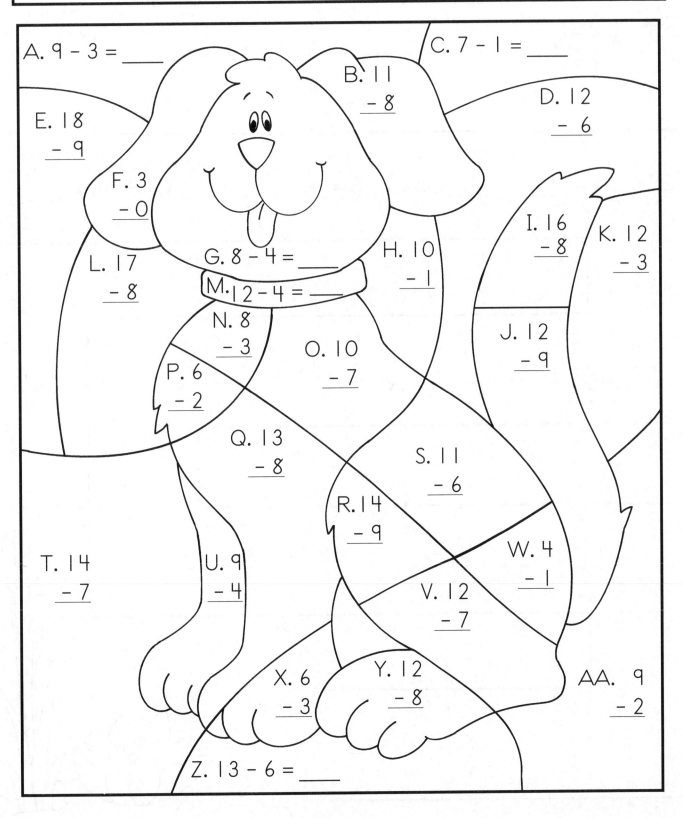

A. 9 – 3 = ___

C. 7 – 1 = ___

B. 11
– 8

D. 12
– 6

E. 18
– 9

F. 3
– 0

L. 17
– 8

G. 8 – 4 = ___

M. 12 – 4 = ___

N. 8
– 3

H. 10
– 1

I. 16
– 8

K. 12
– 3

J. 12
– 9

O. 10
– 7

P. 6
– 2

Q. 13
– 8

R. 14
– 9

S. 11
– 6

W. 4
– 1

T. 14
– 7

U. 9
– 4

V. 12
– 7

X. 6
– 3

Y. 12
– 8

AA. 9
– 2

Z. 13 – 6 = ___

Name_____

Subtract to solve the problems. Help the frog find its way to the lilly pad.

A. 13 – 9 = ___   B. 11 – 3 = ___

E. 6 – 3 = ___   D. 14 – 5 = ___   C. 9 – 9 = ___

F. 10 – 4 = ___   G. 18 – 9 = ___

I. 9 – 7 = ___   H. 16 – 8 = ___

J. 15 – 8 = ___   K. 8 – 7 = ___

Name_____

Add to solve the problems. Help the clown find his car.

A. 5 + 4 = ___   B. 6 + 9 = ___

E. 9 + 4 = ___   D. 8 + 2 = ___   C. 7 + 7 = ___

F. 5 + 6 = ___   G. 9 + 9 = ___   H. 6 + 6 = ___

K. 6 + 1 = ___   J. 0 + 6 = ___   I. 8 + 8 = ___

L. 9 + 8 = ___   M. 5 + 5 = ___

Add to solve the problems in the problem list. Use + and = to find the same problems in the puzzle. Circle the hidden problems.

Problem List

8 + 7 = ___	9 + 5 = ___	5 + 5 = ___	7 + 3 = ___	8 + 6 = ___
6 + 7 = ___	7 + 6 = ___	8 + 8 = ___	9 + 9 = ___	2 + 8 = ___
7 + 4 = ___	5 + 9 = ___		6 + 5 = ___	6 + 9 = ___
9 + 8 = ___	9 + 2 = ___		4 + 6 = ___	6 + 6 = ___

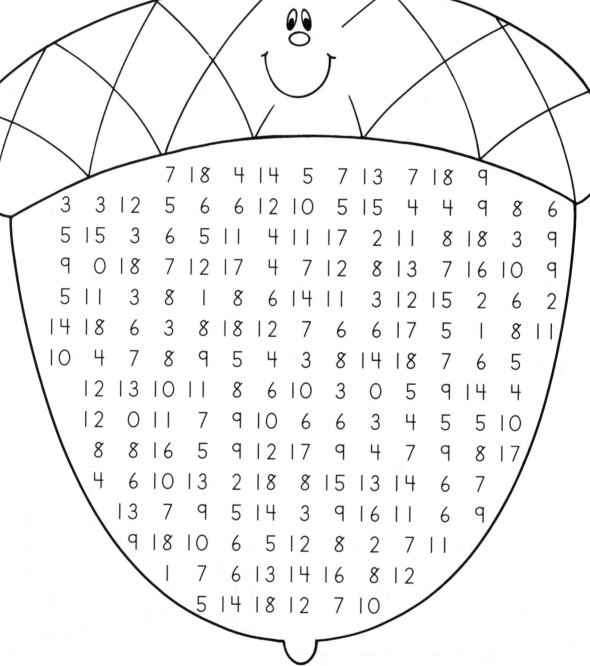

```
        7 18  4 14  5  7 13  7 18  9
     3  3 12  5  6  6 12 10  5 15  4  4  9  8  6
     5 15  3  6  5 11  4 11 17  2 11  8 18  3  9
     9  0 18  7 12 17  4  7 12  8 13  7 16 10  9
     5 11  3  8  1  8  6 14 11  3 12 15  2  6  2
    14 18  6  3  8 18 12  7  6  6 17  5  1  8 11
    10  4  7  8  9  5  4  3  8 14 18  7  6  5
    12 13 10 11  8  6 10  3  0  5  9 14  4
    12  0 11  7  9 10  6  6  3  4  5  5 10
     8  8 16  5  9 12 17  9  4  7  9  8 17
        4  6 10 13  2 18  8 15 13 14  6  7
          13  7  9  5 14  3  9 16 11  6  9
             9 18 10  6  5 12  8  2  7 11
                1  7  6 13 14 16  8 12
                   5 14 18 12  7 10
```

Name_____

Subtract to solve the problems in the problem list. Then use – and = to find the same problems hidden across and down in the puzzle. Circle the hidden problems.

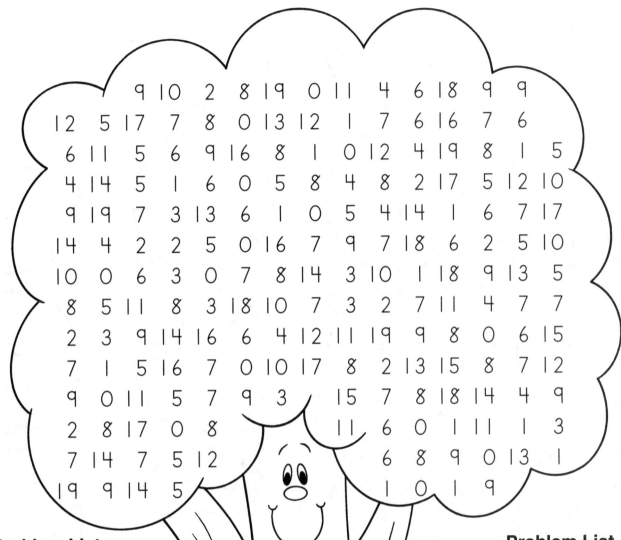

9	10	2	8	19	0	11	4	6	18	9	9			
12	5	17	7	8	0	13	12	1	7	6	16	7	6	
6	11	5	6	9	16	8	1	0	12	4	19	8	1	5
4	14	5	1	6	0	5	8	4	8	2	17	5	12	10
9	19	7	3	13	6	1	0	5	4	14	1	6	7	17
14	4	2	2	5	0	16	7	9	7	18	6	2	5	10
10	0	6	3	0	7	8	14	3	10	1	18	9	13	5
8	5	11	8	3	18	10	7	3	2	7	11	4	7	7
2	3	9	14	16	6	4	12	11	19	9	8	0	6	15
7	1	5	16	7	0	10	17	8	2	13	15	8	7	12
9	0	11	5	7	9	3		15	7	8	18	14	4	9
2	8	17	0	8				11	6	0	1	11	1	3
7	14	7	5	12					6	8	9	0	13	1
19	9	14	5						1	0	1	9		

Problem List

11 – 5 = ____

13 – 8 = ____

12 – 7 = ____   15 – 7 = ____

5 – 0 = ____   11 – 8 = ____

16 – 7 = ____

15 – 8 = ____

10 – 8 = ____

Problem List

10 – 2 = ____

12 – 8 = ____

18 – 9 = ____   11 – 4 = ____

12 – 9 = ____   10 – 7 = ____

4 – 2 = ____

9 – 2 = ____

6 – 4 = ____

Add or subtract to solve the problems.

A. 0
 + 3

B. 4
 + 7

C. 3
 + 4

D. 9
 + 6

E. 7
 + 8

F. 9
 + 4

G. 5
 + 1

H. 8
 + 4

I. 1
 + 4

J. 1
 + 8

K. 13
 − 5

L. 16
 − 7

M. 18
 − 9

N. 5
 − 2

O. 8
 − 7

P. 12
 − 6

Q. 14
 − 8

R. 8
 − 0

S. 15
 − 9

T. 11
 − 8

Name_____

Add or subtract to solve the problems.

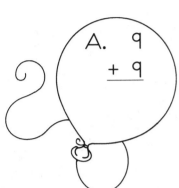

A. 9
+ 9

B. 5
– 0

C. 9
– 1

D. 4
– 0

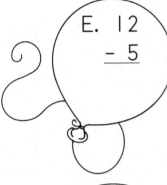

E. 12
– 5

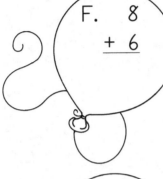

F. 8
+ 6

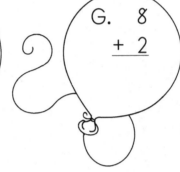

G. 8
+ 2

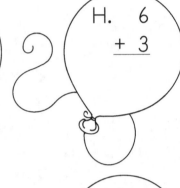

H. 6
+ 3

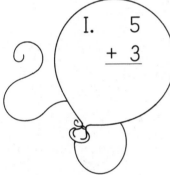

I. 5
+ 3

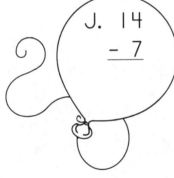

J. 14
– 7

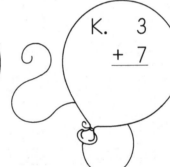

K. 3
+ 7

L. 11
– 7

M. 1
+ 8

N. 4
+ 5

O. 9
– 5

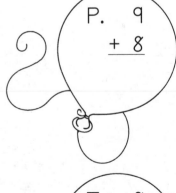

P. 9
+ 8

Q. 7
– 6

R. 4
+ 3

S. 5
– 2

T. 8
– 1

Add or subtract to solve the problems.

A. 8
  − 0

B. 4
  + 9

C. 5
  + 6

D. 14
  − 6

E. 7
  + 7

F. 3
  + 8

G. 17
  − 8

H. 10
  − 3

I. 4
  + 0

J. 16
  − 9

K. 2
  + 9

L. 7
  + 8

M. 9
  − 3

N. 6
  + 7

O. 1
  + 7

P. 4
  + 5

Q. 12
  − 5

R. 8
  + 9

S. 2
  + 4

T. 13
  − 8

U. 11
  − 2

V. 6
  + 8

W. 1
  + 0

X. 18
  − 9

Y. 14
  − 5

Z. 3
  + 9

AA. 15
  − 6

BB. 8
  + 2

CC. 11
  − 7

DD. 5
  + 8

EE. 13
  − 4

FF. 8
  + 4

GG. 6
  + 9

HH. 16
  − 8

II. 1
  + 8

Name_____

Add or subtract to solve the problems.

A. 2
   + 7

B. 8
   + 2

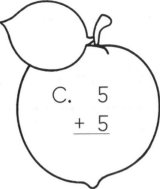
C. 5
   + 5

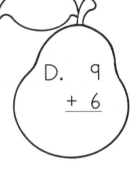
D. 9
   + 6

E. 10
   − 1

F. 13
   − 9

G. 7
   − 7

H. 18
   − 9

I. 7
   + 5

J. 5
   + 4

K. 8
   + 8

L. 9
   + 8

M. 15
   − 8

N. 8
   − 5

O. 17
   − 9

P. 13
   − 8

Q. 5
   + 9

Name_____

Add to solve the problems. Then, use the key to color the picture.

Key
13 = yellow   17 = red   14 = orange   15 = blue   11 = pink   16 = light purple

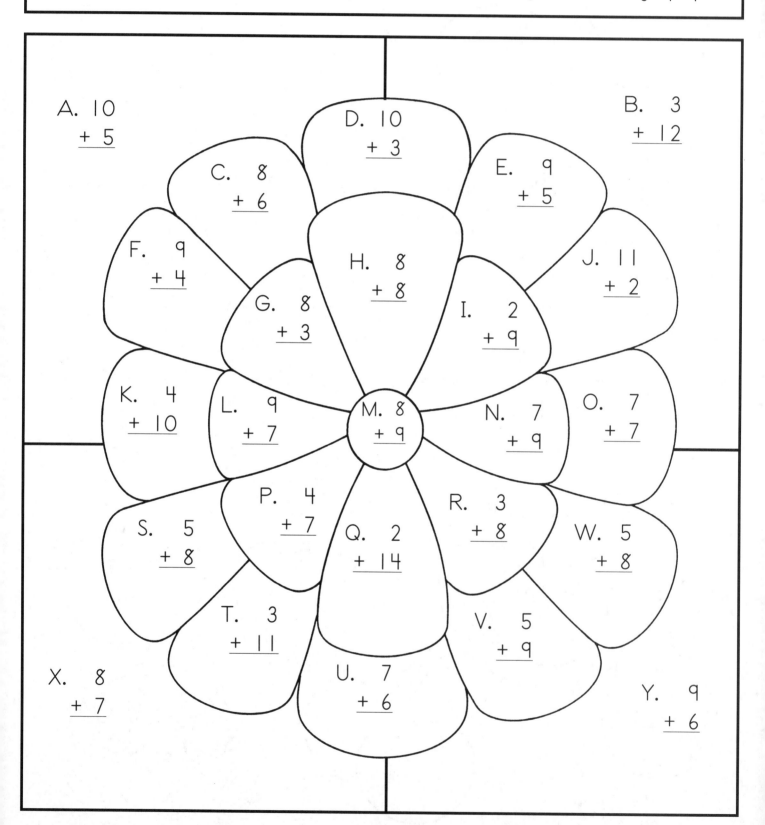

A. 10
+ 5

D. 10
+ 3

B. 3
+ 12

C. 8
+ 6

E. 9
+ 5

F. 9
+ 4

H. 8
+ 8

J. 11
+ 2

G. 8
+ 3

I. 2
+ 9

K. 4
+ 10

L. 9
+ 7

M. 8
+ 9

N. 7
+ 9

O. 7
+ 7

P. 4
+ 7

R. 3
+ 8

S. 5
+ 8

Q. 2
+ 14

W. 5
+ 8

T. 3
+ 11

V. 5
+ 9

X. 8
+ 7

U. 7
+ 6

Y. 9
+ 6

Add or subtract to solve the problems.

A. 7 + 7	B. 6 + 9	C. 4 + 8	D. 3 + 9	E. 9 + 5	F. 7 + 8

G. 6 + 6	H. 8 + 4	I. 6 + 8	J. 9 + 6	K. 5 + 7	L. 9 + 3

M. 4 + 5	N. 16 − 7	O. 9 − 0	P. 2 + 7	Q. 15 − 6	R. 13 − 4

S. 6 + 3	T. 9 + 0	U. 1 + 8	V. 14 − 5	W. 11 − 2	X. 3 + 6

Y. 0 + 9	Z. 18 − 9	AA. 12 − 3	BB. 5 + 4	CC. 17 − 8	DD. 7 + 2

Name_____

Add or subract to solve the problems.

A.   9
   + 1

B.   6
   + 3

C.   7
   + 3

D. 16
   − 8

E. 18
   − 9

F.   5
   + 4

G.   7
   + 9

H. 15
   − 7

I.   9
   + 3

J.   0
   + 8

K.   6
   + 6

L. 14
   − 6

M. 12
   − 4

N.   3
   + 5

O.   9
   + 7

P.   8
   + 8

Q. 13
   − 5

R. 17
   − 9

S.   4
   + 8

T.   7
   + 3

Name_____

Subtract to solve the problems.

A. 15
  − 6

B. 18
  − 9

C. 10
  − 5

D. 12
  − 9

E. 12
  − 6

F. 13
  − 7

G. 11
  − 5

H. 15
  − 7

I. 9
  − 9

J. 14
  − 9

K. 15
  − 8

L. 16
  − 8

M. 10
  − 8

N. 14
  − 7

O. 13
  − 5

P. 17
  − 9

Q. 11
  − 2

R. 10
  − 6

S. 16
  − 7

T. 11
  − 4

U. 16
  − 8

V. 12
  − 4

W. 13
  − 4

X. 14
  − 5

Y. 18
  − 6

Z. 16
  − 4

Name_____

Add to solve the problems.

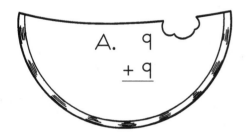
A. 9
+ 9

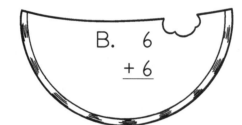
B. 6
+ 6

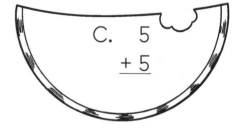
C. 5
+ 5

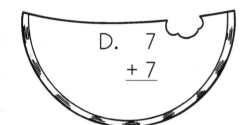
D. 7
+ 7

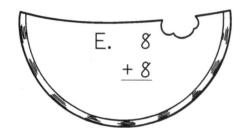
E. 8
+ 8

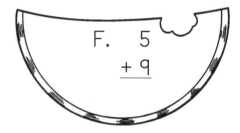
F. 5
+ 9

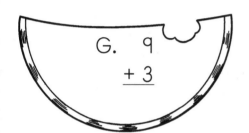
G. 9
+ 3

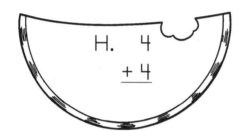
H. 4
+ 4

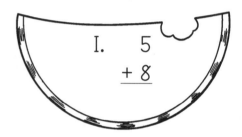
I. 5
+ 8

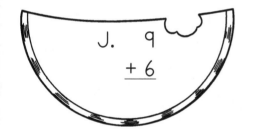
J. 9
+ 6

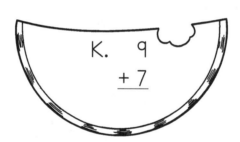
K. 9
+ 7

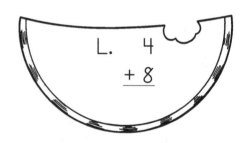
L. 4
+ 8

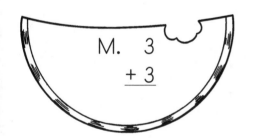
M. 3
+ 3

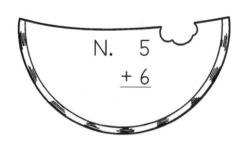
N. 5
+ 6

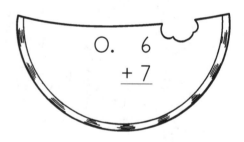
O. 6
+ 7

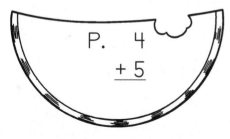
P. 4
+ 5

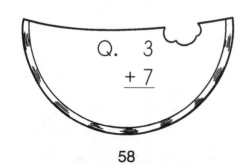
Q. 3
+ 7

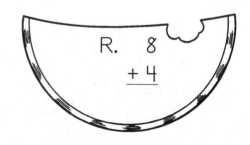
R. 8
+ 4

Add to solve the problems in the problem list. Use + and = to find the same problems hidden across and down in the puzzle.

Problem List					
7 + 4= ___	5 + 8= ___	9 + 4= ___	6 + 8= ___	7 + 5= ___	3 + 7= ___
9 + 9= ___	9 + 7= ___	9 + 6= ___	5 + 5= ___	6 + 7= ___	8 + 7= ___
8 + 8= ___	7 + 7= ___	4 + 8= ___	3 + 8= ___	8 + 5= ___	8 + 3= ___

```
 6  9  7  4 11  1  8  6  5  5 10  3  8
 8  5 18  8  6 11  2  6  7 13  3  2  8
14  8 16  7  8  7  5 12  2 10  0  4 16
 4 13  3 15  0  9 16  4  9 15  8 14  6
14  3 13  5  3  7 14  6  4  8 12  2  7
 3  8 11  1  9 16  9  5 18  3  7 10  0
 5  6  7  7 14  9 16 10  9  4 13  3  5
 5  4 13 10  9 12  7  4  8  5 12 11  6
 2  9  4 17  1 11  4  6 14  3 19 17
17 15 13 15  9  9  9 18  2 10  5  3
 3  6  9  6 15  8 17  9  4  6  9  1
 9  0  7  4  8 10  5  4 11  7  0  2
11 15  6  9  3  3  0  2  9  8  5 13
    8  9  7 11  3 15  3 16  9  2  8
```

Subtract to solve the problems in the problem list. Use − and = to find the same problems hidden across and down in the puzzle. Circle the hidden problems.

Problem List

13 − 5 = _____	13 − 9 = _____
10 − 8 = _____	12 − 8 = _____
9 − 9 = _____	16 − 7 = _____
15 − 6 = _____	4 − 2 = _____
14 − 7 = _____	9 − 1 = _____
12 − 5 = _____	15 − 8 = _____
18 − 9 = _____	10 − 6 = _____
10 − 7 = _____	11 − 4 = _____
	12 − 9 = _____

```
         18  16   8   4   9    9   0   3  11
          9   7   5   9  19   14  12   8   4  11
      6   8   9  10  13   14   7   6   0  11   2  15
  4   7  12  15   1  17    3  10   6   4   4   9   8
 13   0  18  10  15   8    9   7  10  13   7   4   7   3
  9   0   3   2   6   6    1  12   9   3   8  11   7  10
 18  14   4   5   9  14    4   2   2   6  13  16   8   4
  8   1   1   8  16   7    9   9  11   7  10   5  14   5
  2   0  13  12   4  14    7   7   4  13   7   7  18  13
 12  18   5   5   0   2    6   2  16   9   3   1  16   9
 16  19   8   7   9   1    8   8   8   4   3  18  17   4
 13   7   2   7  10   8    2   3   1   8   4   5   9
```

Answer Key

Page 1 **Addition Facts:** O to 18
A. 8, 2, 9, 2, 5, 13, 11, 8, 7, 11
B. 1, 13, 16, 8, 7, 8, 4, 8, 7, 6
C. 10, 6, 8, 7, 10, 15, 11, 7, 10, 0
D. 6, 7, 9, 15, 12, 5, 15, 5, 9, 9
E. 10, 6, 16, 1, 5, 5, 8, 3, 14, 13
F. 4, 2, 5, 12, 11, 18, 10, 9, 8, 14
G. 14, 10, 13, 12, 14, 8, 7, 4, 12, 14
H. 9, 9, 9, 13, 7, 11, 11, 13, 9, 6
I. 3, 17, 6, 3, 17, 9, 4, 15, 11, 12
J. 10, 6, 16, 11, 3, 10, 4, 12, 12, 10

Page 2 **Addition Facts:** O to 18
A. 6, 3, 13, 12, 4, 18, 7, 2, 17, 9
B. 5, 2, 6, 8, 13, 2, 7, 12, 10, 16
C. 9, 8, 8, 7, 15, 4, 16, 7, 11, 5
D. 8, 12, 14, 7, 15, 1, 10, 12, 7, 4
E. 13, 6, 11, 6, 9, 10, 12, 6, 10, 7
F. 8, 12, 11, 8, 1, 9, 6, 17, 9, 10
G. 6, 3, 3, 11, 3, 8, 11, 8, 14, 14
H. 16, 10, 4, 12, 15, 5, 11, 10, 9, 15
I. 4, 9, 7, 14, 5, 9, 13, 0, 13, 13
J. 9, 5, 14, 11, 9, 10, 11, 8, 10, 5

Page 3 **Addition Facts:** O to 18
A. 4, 10, 9, 9, 12, 6, 3, 8, 4, 2
B. 9, 13, 7, 13, 4, 7, 10, 8, 14, 10
C. 10, 1, 8, 0, 16, 8, 8, 11, 9, 6
D. 5, 18, 2, 13, 3, 4, 14, 9, 6, 11
E. 11, 7, 11, 11, 8, 10, 7, 15, 13, 2
F. 5, 14, 6, 9, 12, 5, 17, 15, 3, 10
G. 10, 1, 16, 11, 9, 7, 8, 11, 16, 12
H. 12, 3, 6, 5, 15, 9, 9, 13, 5, 7
I. 4, 11, 12, 5, 15, 13, 14, 8, 9, 14
J. 8, 12, 7, 6, 12, 6, 17, 7, 10, 10

Page 4 **Addition Facts:** O to 18
A. 3, 16, 5, 8, 12, 2, 4, 11, 7, 6
B. 3, 6, 0, 9, 17, 2, 4, 13, 12, 10
C. 14, 9, 16, 7, 10, 8, 8, 11, 2, 13
D. 5, 11, 13, 12, 9, 5, 14, 6, 5, 10
E. 9, 4, 10, 8, 8, 14, 5, 1, 11, 13
F. 10, 15, 10, 7, 4, 7, 12, 12, 16, 6
G. 8, 4, 5, 9, 7, 3, 9, 11, 8, 14
H. 6, 15, 10, 6, 13, 9, 18, 1, 9, 11
I. 15, 7, 6, 10, 14, 8, 7, 12, 17, 8
J. 3, 13, 7, 11, 10, 11, 12, 9, 15, 9

Page 5 **Addition Facts:** O to 18
A. 8, 14, 7, 2, 11, 5, 5, 11, 7, 4
B. 13, 11, 13, 2, 14, 12, 10, 5, 7, 11
C. 10, 3, 13, 7, 9, 1, 10, 4, 11, 10
D. 6, 8, 3, 13, 8, 10, 6, 4, 9, 15
E. 9, 13, 12, 16, 5, 15, 9, 9, 8, 3
F. 12, 14, 7, 12, 9, 17, 17, 6, 1, 12
G. 5, 6, 10, 11, 10, 6, 9, 11, 12, 13
H. 18, 9, 4, 3, 16, 7, 6, 16, 8, 14
I. 8, 0, 14, 11, 15, 8, 10, 10, 15, 9
J. 6, 7, 5, 8, 2, 8, 9, 7, 13, 4

Page 6 **Addition Facts:** O to 18
A. 11, 10, 8, 9, 6, 8, 9, 2, 13, 9
B. 13, 4, 10, 6, 15, 12, 7, 15, 4, 3
C. 0, 13, 10, 8, 1, 15, 7, 9, 14, 11
D. 7, 5, 4, 8, 13, 2, 3, 11, 4, 9
E. 10, 7, 8, 5, 16, 9, 12, 8, 12, 7
F. 9, 10, 4, 9, 10, 7, 13, 6, 11, 7
G. 5, 10, 8, 12, 8, 3, 14, 8, 17, 14
H. 5, 3, 17, 12, 6, 11, 6, 6, 1, 14
I. 13, 11, 11, 10, 12, 11, 7, 15, 18, 5
J. 9, 5, 9, 6, 16, 10, 16, 14, 2, 12

Page 7 **Addition Facts:** O to 18
A. 5, 3, 7, 7, 10, 9, 14, 6, 3, 2
B. 14, 10, 4, 11, 2, 11, 4, 9, 0, 13
C. 12, 17, 7, 13, 6, 8, 15, 10, 6, 10
D. 9, 4, 10, 3, 8, 9, 7, 13, 2, 13
E. 3, 6, 16, 5, 5, 9, 5, 1, 10, 12
F. 7, 1, 10, 7, 8, 6, 11, 16, 14, 5
G. 12, 11, 9, 9, 12, 11, 8, 18, 6, 15
H. 12, 11, 15, 4, 5, 17, 11, 9, 13, 12
I. 8, 6, 12, 15, 9, 4, 8, 10, 11, 10
J. 7, 14, 9, 8, 14, 8, 7, 16, 8, 13

Page 8 **Addition Facts:** O to 18
A. 9, 13, 12, 7, 3, 10, 2, 16, 2, 8
B. 9, 1, 13, 10, 7, 7, 14, 7, 13, 7
C. 15, 4, 10, 0, 12, 10, 7, 17, 5, 11
D. 6, 8, 9, 3, 8, 2, 14, 14, 6, 12
E. 9, 11, 6, 8, 11, 18, 1, 10, 11, 6
F. 12, 4, 9, 5, 5, 16, 10, 17, 7, 15
G. 10, 10, 8, 5, 9, 12, 15, 9, 15, 13
H. 13, 13, 4, 10, 8, 3, 5, 5, 11, 11
I. 6, 9, 11, 6, 8, 11, 12, 9, 3, 14
J. 9, 8, 7, 4, 4, 14, 6, 12, 16, 8

Page 9 **Addition Facts:** O to 18
A. 10, 5, 11, 13, 1   K. 14, 1, 5, 12, 7
B. 7, 12, 9, 5, 7   L. 9, 18, 7, 8, 16
C. 5, 8, 7, 2, 14   M. 8, 12, 16, 9, 12
D. 10, 6, 10, 12, 4   N. 2, 16, 8, 7, 15
E. 17, 6, 4, 9, 9   O. 11, 5, 10, 4, 7
F. 8, 14, 13, 8, 10   P. 6, 13, 3, 14, 6
G. 10, 9, 6, 11, 8   Q. 10, 11, 11, 15, 12
H. 14, 11, 13, 4, 0   R. 9, 4, 9, 11, 13
I. 8, 9, 3, 9, 5   S. 8, 3, 11, 17, 15
J. 3, 7, 12, 2, 15   T. 6, 13, 10, 10, 6

Page 10 **Addition Facts:** O to 18
A. 7, 7, 8, 12, 13   K. 15, 2, 8, 11, 10
B. 12, 6, 14, 4, 2   L. 5, 11, 10, 7, 9
C. 8, 5, 14, 9, 10   M. 8, 15, 3, 9, 4
D. 9, 10, 4, 8, 14   N. 12, 3, 5, 6, 13
E. 12, 11, 16, 10, 12   O. 8, 13, 5, 9, 7
F. 13, 3, 11, 1, 16   P. 6, 0, 13, 9, 9
G. 3, 7, 2, 7, 7   Q. 15, 6, 10, 9, 7
H. 18, 11, 8, 9, 14   R. 4, 16, 17, 14, 11
I. 5, 6, 17, 1, 10   S. 11, 8, 6, 12, 10
J. 10, 12, 6, 13, 4   T. 9, 11, 15, 8, 5

Answer Key

Page 11   Addition Facts: 0 to 18

A. 9, 2, 5, 8, 3
B. 8, 11, 10, 6, 15
C. 4, 9, 13, 11, 2
D. 13, 7, 18, 1, 11
E. 6, 13, 7, 11, 6
F. 13, 1, 6, 15, 4
G. 9, 3, 10, 7, 8
H. 7, 16, 5, 7, 4
I. 8, 12, 6, 10, 8
J. 7, 14, 3, 16, 6

K. 10, 8, 5, 11, 14
L. 16, 8, 5, 14, 15
M. 2, 8, 12, 0, 10
N. 4, 11, 9, 10, 12
O. 8, 11, 12, 12, 11
P. 9, 14, 5, 14, 7
Q. 9, 3, 12, 17, 10
R. 10, 15, 13, 7, 5
S. 17, 4, 9, 12, 10
T. 9, 9, 6, 9, 13

Page 12   Subtraction Facts: 0 to 18

A. 5, 3, 9 5, 6, 1, 6, 0, 9, 7
B. 1, 9, 3, 4, 2, 9, 0, 2, 4, 8,
C. 5, 8, 8, 0, 5, 4, 7, 9, 8, 4
D. 8, 9, 0, 3, 2, 7, 6, 3, 4, 7
E. 0, 9, 1, 1, 3, 1, 1, 4, 5, 8
F. 4, 6, 4, 7, 2, 8, 8, 7, 0, 7
G. 5, 3, 6, 6, 0, 6, 9, 1, 3, 5
H. 8, 7, 6, 1, 2, 9, 2, 0, 9, 3
I. 2, 7, 0, 2, 2, 6, 1, 2, 0, 5
J. 7, 4, 5, 4, 5, 3, 8, 3, 6, 1

Page 13   Subtraction Facts: 0 to 18

A. 7, 2, 9, 6, 6, 9, 8, 1, 0, 0
B. 1, 0, 3, 5, 2, 1, 9, 5, 5, 8
C. 3, 8, 0, 7, 1, 8, 3, 3, 2, 5
D. 5, 8, 0, 7, 3, 5, 7, 9, 1, 2
E. 4, 6, 5, 4, 4, 2, 7, 0, 1, 4
F. 2, 2, 9, 3, 7, 6, 5, 9, 4, 6
G. 2, 0, 6, 9, 1, 8, 3, 0, 7, 8
H. 1, 6, 5, 9, 5, 9, 4, 9, 3, 4
I. 8, 6, 6, 6, 3, 2, 4, 0, 7, 4
J. 2, 8, 4, 1, 8, 3, 7, 0, 7, 1

Page 14   Subtraction Facts: 0 to 18

A. 2, 9, 1, 7, 7, 4, 0, 6, 2, 4
B. 8, 1, 6, 0, 6, 0, 9, 0, 3, 5
C. 4, 9, 5, 9, 5, 4, 8, 9, 2, 4
D. 5, 8, 2, 5, 9, 2, 6, 0, 3, 2
E. 5, 2, 3, 3, 1, 7, 7, 1, 3, 9
F. 0, 1, 1, 7, 5, 3, 0, 9, 7, 0
G. 6, 7, 7, 0, 4, 6, 6, 3, 1, 2
H. 5, 2, 3, 6, 8, 8, 7, 1, 5, 9
I. 1, 6, 8, 8, 4, 1, 9, 4, 8, 2
J. 7, 0, 5, 4, 3, 8, 4, 6, 3, 8

Page 15   Subtraction Facts: 0 to 18

A. 5, 3, 4, 4, 8, 6, 9, 0, 4, 4
B. 9, 1, 9, 1, 7, 0, 6, 8, 6, 3
C. 6, 2, 0, 4, 1, 0, 3, 5, 8, 2
D. 0, 3, 2, 8, 5, 9, 5, 6, 0, 2
E. 4, 1, 3, 4, 7, 2, 7, 7, 6, 4
F. 3, 7, 6, 9, 0, 9, 3, 9, 0, 9
G. 8, 1, 3, 7, 0, 4, 1, 3, 9, 6
H. 2, 0, 7, 1, 6, 5, 5, 8, 7, 9
I. 2, 6, 5, 2, 5, 5, 2, 8, 1, 8
J. 7, 1, 2, 5, 4, 8, 3, 1, 7, 8

Page 16   Subtraction Facts: 0 to 18

A. 4, 1, 9, 8, 2, 5, 6, 8, 4, 3
B. 4, 8, 4, 7, 1, 5, 2, 8, 2, 8
C. 8, 0, 7, 3, 7, 8, 5, 6, 7, 6
D. 0, 5, 5, 3, 4, 5, 7, 0, 3, 9
E. 0, 1, 0, 8, 1, 9, 1, 9, 2, 5
F. 0, 4, 1, 1, 2, 9, 6, 3, 0, 1
G. 2, 8, 6, 1, 9, 4, 2, 2, 3, 7
H. 2, 6, 6, 0, 6, 3, 4, 9, 6, 9
I. 5, 4, 3, 7, 7, 5, 9, 9, 8, 2
J. 0, 7, 5, 3, 4, 0, 6, 3, 1, 7

Page 17   Subtraction Facts: 0 to 18

A. 5, 6, 0, 7, 1, 1, 3, 4, 7, 1
B. 4, 0, 6, 7, 2, 8, 7, 4, 2, 6
C. 4, 6, 2, 7, 3, 3, 0, 6, 0, 7
D. 6, 2, 8, 3, 6, 5, 8, 5, 8, 3
E. 6, 3, 8, 8, 7, 3, 9, 8, 1, 1
F. 2, 5, 4, 8, 1, 6, 5, 9, 0, 1
G. 7, 1, 8, 8, 4, 4, 0, 9, 0, 9
H. 0, 4, 9, 4, 9, 4, 5, 1, 0, 2
I. 9 7, 2, 5, 2, 9, 2, 9, 0, 3
J. 3, 5, 5, 5, 7, 6, 2, 9, 3, 1

Page 18   Subtraction Facts: 0 to 18

A. 9, 3, 0, 9, 6, 2, 6, 6, 3, 1
B. 4, 3, 9, 5, 5, 7, 5, 1, 9, 8
C. 3, 0, 4, 6, 2, 2, 2, 9, 3, 4
D. 2, 7, 7, 8, 0, 4, 6, 7, 0, 1
E. 3, 3, 5, 4, 9, 4, 1, 6, 6, 8
F. 1, 3, 1, 1, 8, 1, 7, 3, 3, 5
G. 5, 0, 5, 9, 9, 7, 5, 7, 4, 8
H. 0, 4, 0, 5, 2, 1, 9, 6, 7, 2
I. 0, 8, 8, 7, 9, 2, 8, 7, 0, 6
J. 6, 8, 4, 5, 2, 8, 1, 4, 0, 2

Page 19   Subtraction Facts: 0 to 18

A. 1, 3, 1, 6, 2, 7, 0, 3, 2, 3
B. 0, 4, 8, 3, 8, 7, 3, 4, 7, 3
C. 6, 5, 6, 2, 4, 7, 0, 9, 1, 2
D. 4, 9, 1, 9, 0, 9, 8, 3, 1, 3
E. 5, 0, 9, 1, 4, 8, 8, 5, 7, 4
F. 4, 2, 2, 0, 9, 4, 0, 5, 5, 6
G. 5, 5, 1, 7, 0, 9, 5, 2, 6, 3
H. 8, 1, 6, 6, 7, 2, 8, 3, 1, 4
I. 9, 6, 6, 1, 4, 0, 5, 8, 2, 8
J. 2, 9, 5, 7, 7, 9, 0, 6, 8, 7

Page 20   Subtraction Facts: 0 to 18

A. 2, 5, 0, 1, 6
B. 5, 1, 4, 0, 8
C. 4, 1, 5, 8, 6
D. 2, 6, 6, 6, 1
E. 3, 2, 7, 1, 5
F. 9, 3, 6, 5, 8
G. 7, 2, 8, 2, 3
H. 5, 0, 3, 8, 2
I. 1, 8, 7, 6, 7
J. 9, 0, 9, 2, 3

K. 7, 1, 0, 4, 1
L. 0, 4, 9, 7, 8
M. 7, 9, 3, 9, 2
N. 3, 4, 9, 9, 0
O. 4, 9, 0, 3, 3
P. 4, 8, 7, 5, 2
Q. 6, 6, 7, 6, 4
R. 1, 5, 8, 0, 8
S. 3, 9, 4, 7, 0
T. 5, 4, 1, 2, 5

Answer Key

Page 21   Subtraction Facts: 0 to 18

A. 6, 9, 2, 5, 0
B. 5, 2, 5, 4, 2
C. 6, 7, 6, 8, 3
D. 1, 3, 2, 3, 1
E. 8, 7, 9, 5, 2
F. 0, 6, 8, 0, 3
G. 8, 9, 3, 1, 3
H. 6, 2, 3, 6, 0
I. 2, 7, 9, 7, 8
J. 1, 4, 3, 2, 1

K. 4, 9, 9, 6, 6
L. 4, 3, 0, 6, 0
M. 2, 8, 6, 8, 8
N. 3, 0, 4, 4, 5
O. 8, 9, 4, 9, 7
P. 9, 1, 4, 7, 5
Q. 9, 4, 1, 7, 5
R. 1, 5, 7, 0, 1
S. 4, 5, 7, 0, 5
T. 7, 2, 1, 8, 0

Page 22   Subtraction Facts: 0 to 18

A. 5, 3, 2, 3, 5
B. 7, 3, 7, 5, 3
C. 9, 6, 1, 7, 1
D. 0, 5, 4, 0, 2
E. 9, 6, 4, 9, 7
F. 1, 9, 4, 4, 6
G. 8, 1, 3, 3, 2
H. 6, 0, 0, 1, 5
I. 9, 6, 7, 3, 7
J. 2, 0, 8, 0, 1

K. 8, 1, 6, 2, 1
L. 6, 9, 4, 1, 7
M. 8, 8, 8, 0, 4
N. 2, 5, 5, 6, 2
O. 4, 5, 9, 6, 9
P. 0, 3, 8, 1, 7
Q. 4, 7, 6, 9, 7
R. 4, 0, 8, 3, 4
S. 5, 0, 2, 8, 3
T. 2, 9, 2, 5, 8

Page 23   Subtraction Facts: 0 to 18

A. 9, 4, 10, 7, 9, 17, 3, 6, 13, 9
B. 3, 6, 4, 5, 2, 6, 12, 8, 4, 0
C. 3, 1, 15, 1, 9, 11, 10, 3, 8, 10
D. 0, 11, 2, 9, 13, 0, 8, 6, 7, 5
E. 6, 9, 5, 4, 8, 6, 4, 13, 16, 3
F. 2, 2, 12, 5, 10, 9, 1, 9, 10, 1
G. 8, 15, 5, 7, 12, 3, 2, 7, 14, 7
H. 8, 2, 4, 7, 1, 6, 9, 4, 3, 8
I. 5, 0, 5, 5, 11, 14, 1, 11, 0, 4
J. 7, 9, 8, 16, 8, 2, 7, 6, 8, 7

Page 24   Addition and Subtraction Facts: 0 to 18

A. 9, 9, 4, 5, 9, 5, 5, 10, 4, 17
B. 9, 10, 10, 5, 8, 10, 3, 13, 5, 6
C. 14, 2, 0, 4, 9, 2, 13, 7, 6, 4
D. 1, 7, 14, 5, 0, 3, 7, 0, 7, 3
E. 9, 4, 3, 10, 8, 6, 12, 1, 5, 8
F. 2, 12, 7, 8, 6, 1, 9, 0, 16, 13
G. 7, 4, 1, 11, 15, 6, 9, 5, 15, 2
H. 9, 2, 6, 3, 2, 3, 5, 5, 0, 6
I. 9, 14, 6, 0, 12, 8, 3, 6, 7, 3
J. 8, 8, 13, 8, 1, 2, 9, 13, 16, 9

Page 25   Addition and Subtraction Facts: 0 to 18

A. 0, 15, 7, 6, 4, 9, 14, 3, 7, 7
B. 2, 13, 4, 9, 2, 4, 10, 3, 10, 9
C. 12, 6, 16, 11, 0, 4, 2, 1, 13, 5
D. 5, 3, 8, 7, 2, 10, 6, 8, 8, 10
E. 9, 7, 0, 6, 2, 5, 9, 5, 17, 7
F. 4, 1, 7, 1, 8, 5, 3, 0, 12, 9
G. 7, 4, 9, 2, 13, 4, 3, 10, 8, 14
H. 1, 11, 9, 1, 6, 12, 1, 10, 9, 8
I. 7, 3, 0, 12, 10, 6, 9, 5, 1, 6
J. 3, 16, 5, 9, 8, 14, 6, 8, 4, 9

Page 26   Addition and Subtraction Facts: 0 to 18

A. 8, 8, 10, 9, 5, 11, 11, 6, 4, 3
B. 7, 9, 7, 3, 9, 12, 2, 7, 15, 8
C. 1, 4, 9, 8, 0, 8, 9, 2, 9, 6
D. 4, 6, 9, 2, 7, 10, 9, 1, 0, 13
E. 10, 5, 1, 2, 3, 15, 8, 3, 4, 6
F. 4, 9, 7, 11, 0, 14, 2, 8, 5, 6
G. 7, 3, 13, 1, 5, 5, 11, 1, 0, 7
H. 5, 2, 1, 17, 14, 1, 6, 14, 6, 12
I. 3, 0, 4, 6, 5, 2, 13, 7, 9, 3
J. 5, 12, 3, 11, 9, 9, 8, 8, 15, 15

Page 29
A. 9   B. 12   C. 10
D. 8   E. 7   F. 12
G. 4   H. 18   I. 11
J. 13   K. 10   L. 7
M. 14   N. 10   O. 10
P. 13   Q. 9
R. 10   S. 16

Page 30
A. 7   B. 9   C. 13   D. 9
E. 7   F. 14   G. 13   H. 9
I. 0   J. 11   K. 2   L. 11
M. 17   N. 12
O. 9   P. 1

Page 31
A. 10   B. 8   C. 13   D. 8   E. 15   F. 18
G. 13   H. 17   I. 14   J. 13   K. 13   L. 4
M. 9   N. 15   O. 14   P. 11   Q. 10
R. 16   S. 12   T. 11   U. 12

Page 32
A. 0   B. 1   C. 9   D. 8
E. 0   F. 4   G. 9
H. 7   I. 6   J. 5   K. 3
L. 6   M. 6   N. 3
O. 18   P. 6   Q. 4   R. 7

Page 33
A. 10   B. 10   C. 10   D. 10
E. 14   F. 8   G. 8   H. 10
I. 14   J. 8   K. 8   L. 8
M. 12   N. 18   O. 14   P. 14   Q. 12
R. 12   S. 6   T. 6   U. 6   V. 6
W. 6   X. 6

Page 34
A. 8   B. 8
C. 7   D. 7
E. 3   F. 8   G. 7   H. 5
I. 7   J. 7   K. 4   L. 3   M. 7
N. 3   O. 9   P. 7   Q. 7
R. 7   S. 5   T. 3   U. 4
V. 8   W. 7   X. 8
Y. 7

Page 35
A. 10   G. 9
B. 12   H. 12
C. 6   I. 18
D. 4   J. 7
E. 8   K. 15
F. 13   L. 5

Answer Key

Page 36
A. 8   B. 5
E. 17   D. 12   C. 15
F. 9   G. 4   H. 13
K. 11   J. 16   I. 18
L. 14   M. 10

Page 37

```
 7+4=11  8  5                    8 21
 5  8 14  7 18        4 14  5    7  0
 3  9 12  5  5        4 16 15    5  3
 7  4 11 17  2  6+8=14  3  9+6=15  5  7
 4  7  5+8=13  8 16  8    7 15  3  8  1
 2 11  3 12 18  2  6  7  7 14 18  3  3  8
 4+7=16  6 17  3  1 15  0 10  4  7  8  1
 4  3+9=12 18  7  6  5 15 12  1 10 11  1
 7 13  3  5+5=10  8+4=12  0 11  1  5
15  6 17  8  4  5  7 12  6  7  3  5  9  2
 0  9  6 15  7  9 18 10  4  6  7 14  9  1
 8 15 12  7  6+7=13  7  2 10  7  3  1
 8+8=16  4  9+7=8 10  6  5 12
 2  8 16 11 10  4  9  3 14 16  8
 5  7+5=12  5 14 18 17  8  0  3  6
16  4+9=13  2  0 12 11  0  8
```

Page 38

```
11 16  9 14  5  9 10-5=5  7  4 12
 2  7  9-9=0  9  8  6 12    7-2=5  8
16  9  8 13  0  9 12  1  8    9-3=6  8 13
 4  0 10  9  7 16-7=9 16  7  9 17  4  5
 7 11 12  4  8  7  8  9  7 18 13  8  8  4  9
13 18-9=9  1  8 16 12-3=9 18  1  9  8 12
 6  9 10  3  7  8  9  0 10-3=7 10  5 14
 9  7  3 18  1 10 11 14  7 13 15  9  6
11-4=7  8  7  9  0  5  9  3  0  8  8
17  4  3  0  6  0 16  1 12    4
14  8  9  5 18 13-5=8  1
```

Page 39
A. 13   B. 15   C. 12
D. 10   E. 16   F. 17   G. 13
H. 10   I. 18   J. 11   K. 8
L. 14   M. 9   N. 12   O. 11

Page 40
A. 11   B. 12   C. 16   D. 14
E. 18   F. 17   G. 14   H. 8
I. 13   J. 13   K. 0   L. 5
M. 9   N. 9   O. 9   P. 5
Q. 8   R. 3   S. 3
T. 0   U. 7   V. 8

Page 41
A. 8   B. 9   C. 6   D. 4   E. 2
F. 13   G. 9   H. 15   I. 0   J. 6
K. 6   L. 1   M. 11   N. 7   O. 9
P. 15   Q. 7   R. 8   S. 9   T. 14
U. 8   V. 14   W. 3   X. 7   Y. 10
Z. 8   AA. 12   BB. 10
CC. 5   DD. 6   EE. 16

Page 42
A. 8   B. 11   C. 18
D. 11   E. 6   F. 10   G. 6
H. 7   I. 9   J. 2   K. 6
L. 5   M. 1   N. 13   O. 11
P. 3   Q. 7   R. 10   S. 13

Page 43
A. 4   B. 9
C. 4   D. 4   E. 4   F. 14   G. 9
H. 10   I. 4   J. 6
K. 10   L. 10   M. 12   N. 6   O. 4
P. 4   Q. 6
R. 9   S. 12   T. 12   V. 12   W. 9
X. 6   Y. 4   Z. 4

Page 44
A. 7   B. 7   C. 7   D. 7   E. 7
F. 8   G. 8   H. 8
I. 7   J. 9   K. 14   L. 13   M. 14
N. 9   O. 7   P. 9   Q. 8   R. 8
S. 14   T. 13   U. 14   V. 9   W. 8
X. 9   Y. 13   Z. 9
AA. 14   BB. 14
CC. 9   DD. 8   EE. 9

Page 45
A. 6   B. 3   C. 6   D. 6
E. 9   F. 3   G. 4   H. 9   I. 8
J. 3   K. 9
L. 9   M. 8   N. 5   O. 3
P. 4   Q. 5   R. 5   S. 5
T. 7   U. 5   V. 5   W. 3
X. 3   Y. 4   Z. 7   AA. 7

Page 46
A. 4   B. 8
E. 3   D. 9   C. 0
F. 6   G. 9
I. 2   H. 8
J. 7   K. 1

Page 47
A. 9   B. 15
E. 13   D. 10   C. 14
F. 11   G. 18   H. 12
K. 7   J. 6   I. 16
L. 17   M. 10

Page 48

```
          7 18  4 14  5  7 13  7 18  9
 3  3 12  5  6+6=12 10  5 15    4  4  8  6
 5 15  3  6+5=11  4 11 17  2 11  8  8  3
 9  0 18  7 12 17  4  7 12  8  7 16 10  9
 5 11  3  8  8+6=14 11  3 12 15  2  8 11
14 18  6  3  8 18 12  7  6  8  7  5  1  8
10  4  7  8  9  7  3  8 14 18  7  6
12 13 10 11  8  4  7  6    5+9=14
12  0 11 12  7  3  4  5+5=10
 8+8=16  5  9 12 17  6  4  9+8=17
 4  6 10 13  2 18  8 15 13 14  6
13  7  9+5=14  3  9 16 11  6  9
 9 18 10  6  5 12  8  7  7 11
 1  7+6=13 14 16  8 12
 5 14 18 12  7 10
```

Page 49

```
       9 10-2=8 19  0 11  4  6 18-9=9
12  5 17  7  8  0 13 12  1  7  6 16  7  6
 6 11-5=6  9 16  1  0  2  4 19  8  1  5
 4 14  5  9  6  3  1  0  5  4 17  5  2 10
 9 19  7  3 13  6  1  0  5  4  7  1
14  4-2=2  5  0 16-7=9  7 18  6  2 10
10  0  6  3  0  7  8 14  3 10  1 18  9 13 10
 8  5  1-8=3  8 10-7=3  2  7 11-4=7  1
 2  3  9 14 16  6  4 12 11 19  8  0  6 15
 7  1  5 16  7  0 10 17  8  2 13 15-8=7  2
 9  0 11  5  7  9  3 15-7=8 18 14  4  9
 4  8 17 10  8                     3
 7 14  7  5 10                  6  8  9  0 13  1
19  9 14  5              1  0  1  9
```